TYBURN

TYBURN

The Story of
London's Gallows

ROBERT BARD

AMBERLEY

First published 2012

Amberley Publishing
The Hill, Stroud
Gloucestershire, GL5 4EP

www.amberley-books.com

British Library Cataloguing in Publication Data.
A catalogue record for this book is available from the British Library.

ISBN 978 1 4456 0646 0

Typesetting and origination by Amberley Publishing
Printed in Great Britain

Contents

To Mildred Marks

Introduction

The rope being put about his neck, he is fastened to the fatal tree when a proper time being allowed for prayer and singing a hymn, the cart is withdrawn and the penitent criminal is turned with a cap over his eyes and left hanging half an hour...These executions are always well attended with so great mobbing and impertinences that you ought to be on your guard when curiosity leads you there. (The Foreigner's Guide to London, 1740).

The word 'Tyburn' has been synonymous for centuries with the place near the junction of the Edgware Road and Oxford Street where criminals were executed by hanging. The history of execution at Tyburn is a history of English law, society, power structure, and a mirror to the nature of how crime, often trivial, was dealt with over a period of over 600 years. The gallows, in earliest times, were seen as a symbol of power. Ironically, in a Christian country, abbots fought with other abbots and the monarch for the right to erect gallows in their districts. It has been commented that 'ecclesiastics, forbidden to shed blood, yet hanged men by the hands of their bailliffs. An abbot, for example, had two parts to fulfil. As an ecclesiastic he gave shelter to thieves, as lord of the manor he hanged them.' The same observer comments: 'the Abbot of Westminster had his servants waiting in Thieving Lane to show thieves the way to sanctuary: on the other hand, he had sixteen gallows in Middlesex alone'.[1] The Abbot of Westminster is recorded as having gallows at Tyburn in a document of 1271.[2]

Tyburn was by no means the only site of execution either during these early times or later on. Another early document tells us that the Abbot of Westminster had gallows in 'Eye [a district of Westminster], Teddington, Knightsbridge, Greenford, Chelsea, Brentford, Paddington,

Iveney, Laleham, Hampstead, Ecclesford, Staines, Haliford, Westbourne, and Shepperton'. As late as the Rocque maps of London 1746, gallows can be seen in a number of parts of London, including Shepherd's Bush Green and Cricklewood. Although Tyburn was one of the primary places of execution between *c.*1108 and 1783, London and its surrounds was literally littered with gallows. It was common to punish felons by executing them at the scene of their crime. This means that there are very few areas of London which did not at some time play host to an execution. There are numerous accounts dating from the sixteenth century onwards describing London's solution to political and criminal unsocials. A nineteenth-century writer called London 'the City of Gallows' and remarked that at whatever point you entered London you would have to pass under a line of gibbets. He writes:

> Pass up the Thames, there were gibbets along the banks … Land at Execution Dock (Wapping), and a gallows was being erected for the punishment of some offender … Enter from the west by Oxford-street, and there was the gallows-tree at Tyburn … Cross any of the heaths, commons, or forests near London, and you would be startled by the creaking of the chains from which some gibbeted highwayman was dropping piecemeal … Nay, the gallows was set up before your own door in every part of the town…[3]

Executions in London were popular with the crowd, from the educated to the London mob. Attendance numbers varied, but typically ranged anywhere between 3,000 and 30,000 persons. A particularly notable event could attract up to 100,000 persons. Diaries and letters of prominent persons of the seventeenth, eighteenth and nineteenth centuries describe what it was like to attend such an event. Pepys, in his diaries, describes attending a number of executions. His diary of 13 October 1660 describes the execution of the regicide Thomas Harrison at Charing Cross. The execution took place at the southern end of what is now Trafalgar Square, on the same spot where the statue of Charles I on horseback stands, facing down Whitehall. Striking is the casual description of seeing a man undergoing the most barbaric judicial sentence available:

> To my Lord's in the morning, where I met with Captain Cuttance, but my Lord not being up, I went to Charing Cross, to see Major-General Harrison hanged, drawn,

and quartered; which was done there, he looked as cheerful as man could do in that condition. He was presently cut down, and his head and heart shown to the people, at which there was great shouts of joy … Thus it was by chance to see the King beheaded at White Hall, and to see the first blood shed in revenge for the blood of the King at Charing Cross. From thence to my Lord's, and took Captain Cuttance and Mr Sheply to the Sun Tavern, and did give them some oysters … within all the afternoon setting up shelves in my study. At night to bed.

Pepys also went to see the death of an acquaintance, Colonel James Turner, but was more concerned about his own discomfort than that of his former friend:

21 January 1664. Up; and after sending my wife to my aunt Wight's to get a place to see Turner hanged, I to the office, where we sat all the morning. And at noon, going to the Change and seeing people flock in that, I enquired and found that Turner was not yet hanged; and so I went among them to Leadenhall Street at the end of Lyme Street, near where the robbery was done, and so to St Mary Axe, where he lived, and there I got for a shilling to stand upon the wheel of a cart, in great pain, above an hour before the execution was done.

The following century saw Horace Walpole, 4th Earl of Orford (1717–97) attending the execution by beheading of the 4th Earl of Kilmarnock at Tower Hill for high treason. The Jacobite Rebellion of 1746 claimed a number of noble victims. Kilmarnock, it seems, when stepping onto the scaffold and confronting his own waiting coffin, became unnerved. When he knelt on the block, he asked the executioner not to strike until he dropped a handkerchief he was holding in his hand. Walpole comments that Killmarnock was much terrified and 'testing' the block several times knelt down at the block but showed a 'visible unwillingness to depart' taking five minutes to drop the handkerchief. The fondness which many minds feel (or rather felt) for these melancholy sights is thus discussed by James Boswell (1740–95), lawyer and diarist, and the multi-talented Dr Samuel Johnson (1709–84): 'I mentioned to him that I had seen the execution of several convicts at Tyburn two days before, and that none of them seemed to be under any concern. Johnson: "Most of them, sir, have never thought at all." Boswell: "But is not the fear of death natural to man?" Johnson: "So much so, sir, that the whole of life is but keeping away the thoughts of it." He then, in a low and earnest tone, talked of his meditating upon the awful hour of his own dissolution, and in what manner he should conduct himself upon that occasion. "I know not," said he, "whether I should wish to have a friend by me, or have it all between God and myself."' Boswell and Johnson look at reasons for attending a hanging in terms of mortality:

Talking of our feeling for the distresses of others – Johnson: 'Why, sir, there is much noise made about it, but it is greatly exaggerated. No, sir, we have a certain degree of feeling to prompt us to do good; more than that Providence does not intend. It would be misery to no purpose.' Boswell: 'But suppose now, sir, that one of your intimate friends were apprehended for an offence for which he might be hanged.' Johnson: 'I should do what I could to bail him, and give him any other assistance; but if he were once fairly hanged, I should not suffer.' Boswell: 'Would you eat your dinner that day, sir?' Johnson: 'Yes, sir; and eat it as if he were eating with me. Why, there's Baretti, who is to be tried for his life to-morrow; friends have risen up for him on every side, yet if he should be hanged, none of them would eat a slice of pudding the less. Sir, that sympathetic feeling goes a very little way in depressing the mind.' (*Old New London*)

By the time we come to the nineteenth century, the nature of execution as a public spectacle was being questioned by some notable persons, including Charles Dickens (1812–70) who attended a number of executions and was disturbed, not only by what he saw, but as to whether the killing of criminals put others off a life of crime.

Dickens wrote:

There never is (and there never was) an execution at the Old Bailey in London, but the spectators include two large classes of thieves – one class who go there as they would go to a dog-fight, or any other brutal sport, for the attraction and excitement of the spectacle; the other who make it a dry matter of business and mix with the crowd solely to pick pockets. Add to these, the dissolute, the drunken, the most idle profligate, and abandoned of both sexes – some moody ill-conditioned minds drawn thither by a fearful interest – and some impelled by curiosity; of whom the greater part are of an age and temperament rendering the gratification of that curiosity highly dangerous to themselves and to society.

The vast majority of those that suffered at Tyburn were London's underclass. It was inevitable that over the centuries a form of carnival and ritual would evolve as those sentenced to die, often many at the same time, were transported from their prison to the place of execution. The myth of 'a good death' and the last speech evolved. In the moments prior to death, those that were previously anonymous could have their moment of fame. A form of 'death literature' evolved recording the final words of the condemned. Interestingly many of these speeches were circulated in the crowd prior to anything having been uttered. There was an element of the Roman gladiator shows. Some of the condemned were able to attract the pity and support of the crowd, going to their death to the sound of cheers and weeping. Others excited crowd hostility and were booed off the platform. Literature evolved, including during the eighteenth and nineteenth centuries' *The Newgate Calendar, or Malefactor's Bloody Register*, which recorded the lives, crimes, and deaths of many criminals, and found itself on many middle-class bookshelves.

Tyburn itself evolved over the centuries, until by the latter part of the eighteenth century a complete ritual had developed in the transport of the victims, usually from Newgate Prison, three miles away, to their final destination. A heaving crowd would accompany the felon in what would be their ultimate pub crawl, bringing many to the gallows totally inebriated. The realities of hanging – the process, the torment, and the disposal of the (usually) deceased victim – will be looked at. As a process, death itself usually came by way of an agonising and slow strangulation. On some rare occasions, the victim came back to life after being cut down from the gallows. There are accounts, which will be looked at, as to what it was like to be hanged and wake up under the surgeon's knife. Although some went to the gallows bravely, the vast majority undoubtedly used the highly ritualised process as a protective shield to help them keep their nerve during their final moments. Many went to the gallows speechless with fear, and some were unable to stand and had to be supported by the hangman and his assistant.

The story of Tyburn raises a number of fascinating questions, such as where exactly were the gallows? What remains to be seen? Victims were often buried in a pit next to the gallows… where are the bodies buried? Apart from a plaque supposedly marking the exact location of the gallows on a traffic island near Edgware Road, there are still other remaining echoes of Tyburn to be found. Apart from the gallows, the location nearby where Speaker's Corner is situated was also a place of execution for the military. During the mid-nineteenth century, a nearby house owner in Connaught Place commented in a letter to *The Times* that workmen had come across numerous quantities of human bones under the pavement. Also, with reference to contemporary accounts, the question of what it was like to attend an execution at Tyburn will be looked at.

The last public execution in England took place on the 26 May 1868. Michael Barrett, an Irish terrorist, became the last man to be publicly hanged in England, before a huge crowd outside Newgate prison, for causing an explosion at Clerkenwell in London which killed Sarah Ann Hodgkinson and six other innocent people. Three days later on 29 May 1868, Parliament passed the Capital Punishment Amendment Act, ending public hanging. Frances Kidder was the last woman to be publicly hanged in Britain, when she was executed at Maidstone at midday on Thursday 2 April 1868. Strangely the last fully public hanging in the British Isles did not take place until 11 August 1875, when Joseph Phillip Le Brun was executed for murder on the island of Jersey. The provisions of the Capital Punishment Amendment Act of 1868 did not apply there.

Ruth Ellis was the last woman to suffer the death penalty in Britain on 13 July 1955. The last hangings in Britain were two carried out simultaneously at 8.00 a.m. on 13 August 1964 at Liverpool's Walton prison and Strangeways prison in Manchester, when Peter Anthony Allen and Gwynne Owen Evans were executed for the murder of John West. One thing that becomes clear from a look at the history of Tyburn is that, during a period when even the hangman could find himself hanged for a crime, there was little by way of deterrent in knowing that a life of crime would lead to the gallows: indeed they were seen by many of London's underclass as an occupational hazard.

1
Tyburn: Origins & Nature of Hanging

The earliest mention of Tyburn in connection with executions is in 1196, when William FitzOsbert, known as Longbeard, was hanged here. It was very likely that the site had been in use for a while, having been established some time after the Norman Conquest. It has been suggested that it was under Henry I (*c.* 1068/9–1135) that the gallows were instituted here, Henry having established law 'by which, if any one was taken in theft or robbery, he should be hanged'.[4]

Tyburn was originally known as 'the Elms'. For the Normans, the elm was the tree of justice. Alfred Marks, in *Tyburn Tree*, an extensive and well-researched history published in 1908, observes that 'Elms Lane, now Elms Mews, a turning out of the Bayswater or Uxbridge Road, probably preserves the name given to the gallows which the abbot of Westminster had at "Westburn" towards the end of the thirteenth century'. Similarly the execution site of Smithfield was known as 'the Elms'. At some date before 1413 the gallows were removed to St Giles, in the vicinity of which the front of the present church of St Giles-in-the-Fields lies, where it continued until its removal to Tyburn. At one time, briefly, the Earl of Oxford set up his own gallows at Tyburn but when challenged, removed them.

In 1220, Henry III (1207–72) ordered the immediate erection of two good gibbets of the best and strongest material for hanging thieves and other malefactors, in the place where gallows were formerly erected, at 'the Elms'. It is probable that they were to replace decaying gallows, suggesting that earlier gallows existed.

The Evolution of Early Hanging
The gallows and the method of hanging a human 'evolved' over the

centuries. Under Elizabeth I (1533–1603) the gallows were modified to allow up to at least twenty-four souls to be simultaneously executed. From time immemorial, death by hanging was actually death by strangulation. The victim would normally be seated on a cart. The cart would pull up beneath the gallows; the noose, usually already placed round his or her neck, would be attached by the hangman or his assistant to the crossbeam, and the cart would be driven away leaving the victim suspended, gasping for breath and thrashing around. Death could take anything from a couple of minutes to over an hour. In some cases, as will be seen, death never even occurred: the victim, after being cut down, revived, leading to concerns as to whether it was legal to re-execute someone who had already been executed. A number of victims escaped in this manner. One writer over a century ago gives what he believes was behind the invention of the 'drop'. The drop was initially a crude method where excess rope was provided, and the victim fell maybe a couple of feet through a trap door, with a view to providing a quicker death. Some contemporaries felt it took the pleasure away from attending executions:

> … the fall would dislocate the neck, and the victim would die otherwise than by strangulation. The 'fall', resulting in immediate death, would deprive the public of what was regarded as the most diverting episode of the piece the tugging by friends at the legs of the suspended man, the thumping him on the chest, rough methods of accelerating his death. But on consideration it seems probable that the State began to have a real concern as to the effect of mere hanging. Moreover, a new art was arising, based on these cases of recovery. Bronchotomy, as applied to victims of the scaffold …[as] early as 1733, [a] Mr Chovet had made such progress in 'preventing the fatal consequences of the Halter' that the State may well have trembled. Here was a new development of smuggling. On the whole it seems safer to conclude that the 'fall' was adopted as a means of bringing to naught these ingenious attempts to rob the State of its due. (Marks)

What Was it Like to be Hanged?

Every now and then those sentenced to death by hanging, essentially slow strangulation, survived their ordeal. An early recorded case was during the reign of Henry III. In 1264 a woman, Ivettade Balsham, was, for an unrecorded crime, hanged at three o'clock one afternoon and cut down from the gallows at sunrise the next morning. She was found to be alive and a pardon was granted. She had been hanging for twelve hours and survived.

Marks comments on a case recorded 'in a little book' published in 1651:

> Newes from the Dead, or a true and exact narration of the miraculous deliverance of Anne Greene, who being executed at Oxford, December 14, 1650, afterwards revived, and by the care of certain Physitians there is now perfectly recovered. Together with the manner of her suffering, and the particular means used for her recovery. Written by a Scholler in Oxford for the satisfaction of a friend who desired to be informed concerning the truth of the businesse. Whereunto are prefixed certain Poems casually written upon that subject.

On 12 December 1705 at Tyburn, one John Smith, condemned at the Old Bailey for burglary, was taken to Tyburn to be executed. About seven minutes after being hanged, a reprieve came. Smith was cut down. The *Old Bailey Chronicle*,[5] states that 'after hanging five minutes and a quarter, a reprieve was brought … The malefactor was cut down and taken with all possible expedition to a public house where proper means was pursued for his recovery, and with so much success that the perfect use of all his faculties was restored in about half an hour.' Another source tells us that 'Smith hanged for about a quarter of an hour'. The executioner, while Smith was hanging, pulled his legs and used other means to put a speedy period to his life. Smith does not seem to have been put off crime by his experience. Remarkably, despite receiving an unconditional pardon he went on to be tried for burglary and acquitted on a point of law and later faced a third charge of burglary, but the prosecutor died and Smith was discharged.[6] A report from Tyburn of November 25 1740:

> Yesterday only five of the Malefactors were executed at Tyburn: two of them, viz., George Wight and Abraham Hancock having obtain'd a Reprieve thro' the Intercession of a Noble Peer. Duel, executed for the Rape, was brought to Surgeons-Hall, in order for Anatomy, but after he was stripp'd and laid on the Board, and one of the Servants was washing him, to be cut up, he perceived Life in him, and found his Breath to come quicker and quicker, on which a Surgeon bled him, and took several Ounces of Blood from him, and in about two Hours he came so much to himself as to sit up in a Chair, groan'd very much, and seem'd in great Agitation, but could not speak: tho' it was the

Opinion of most People if he had been put in a warm Bed and proper Care taken, he would have come to himself. Whether he's now living we know not, but a great Mob assembled at Surgeons-Hall on this Occasion, and according to their Law, he could not be executed again: but according to the Law of the Land, the Sheriffs have a Power to carry him again to Tyburn and execute him, his former sentence, of being hung till he was dead, not having been executed. Its reckon'd his coming to Life was owing to the wrong Disposition of the Halter. (*London Daily Post and General Advertiser*).

On being asked what he remembered of his execution, Duel (or Dewell) did not recollect the actual hanging but said that he had been in a dream; that he dreamed of Paradise, where an angel told him his sins were forgiven. He made a complete recovery. At the next sessions at the Old Bailey he was ordered to be transported for life. Some years before this, the problem of the recovery of persons hanged had received careful attention. In *The Gentleman's Magazine* of 27 April 1733: 'Mr Chovet, a Surgeon, already mentioned, having by frequent Experiments on Dogs, discovered, that opening the Windpipe, would prevent the fatal Consequences of the Halter'. In the same magazine in 1736, two further cases of recovery are mentioned.

On July 26 one Reynolds, a turnpike leveller, was hanged and cut down in the usual course. But as the coffin was being fastened down, Reynolds thrust back the lid, whereupon the executioner was for tying him up again. This however the mob would not suffer. Reynolds was carried to a house where he vomited a quantity of blood, but he died after being made to drink a glass of wine. On September 23rd two men were hanged at Bristol, cut down and put into coffins, when both revived. One died later in the day; what befel the other is not told.

The Gentleman's Magazine, again, in 1767 recorded the execution at Cork, on 24 January, of Patrick Redmond who hung for twenty-eight minutes.

The mob carried off the body to a place appointed, where he was, after five or six hours actually recovered by a surgeon who made the incision in his windpipe called bronchotomy. The poor fellow has since received his pardon, and a genteel collection has been made for him.

Another case was that of Anne Greene, who had been convicted of killing her newly-born child: it is likely the child was born stillborn. An account of the execution tells us:

> She was turned off the ladder, hanging by the neck for the space of almost half an houre, some of her friends in the meantime thumping her on the breast, others hanging with all their weight upon her legs, sometimes lifting her up, and then pulling her doune again with a sudden jerk, thereby the sooner to despatch her out of her pain; insomuch that the Under-sheriff fearing lest thereby they should break the rope forbad them to do so any longer. The body was carried in a coffin into a private house, and showing signs of life: 'a lusty fellow that stood by (thinking to do an act of charity in ridding her out of the small reliques of a painfull life) stamped several times on her breast and stomach with all the force he could.' Dr Petty, the Professor of Anatomy, coming in with another, they set themselves to recover her. They bled her freely, and put her into bed with another woman. After about two hours she could speak 'many words intelligible'. Within a month she was recovered, and went to her friends in the country, taking her coffin with her.

The *Newgate Calendar* of 1774 gives an account of the execution on 19 June 1728 of Margaret Dickenson, who was hanged at Edinburgh. It shows a picture of Margaret sitting up in her coffin. 'After hanging for the usual time, the body was cut down, put into a coffin, and into a cart for carriage to the place of interment. The cart driver stopped in a village to drink, and while so doing saw the lid of the coffin move: at last the woman sat up in her coffin. Most of those present fled in terror, but a gardener, who happened to be there, opened a vein. Within an hour Margaret was put to bed, and on the next day walked home.'

The Procession: Newgate to Tyburn, the Route and Ritual
The following lines, from Swift's *Tom Clinch going to be Hanged*, give a picture of the grim cavalcade wending its way from Newgate to Tyburn in 1727:

> As clever Tom Clinch, while the rabble was bawling,
> Rode stately through Holborn to die in his calling,
> He stopped at the 'George' for a bottle of sack,
> And promised to pay for it—when he came back.
> His waistcoat, and stockings, and breeches were white,

His cap had a new cherry-ribbon to tie ’t;

And the maids to the doors and the balconies ran,

And cried ‘Lack-a-day! he’s a proper young man!’

The Revd Paul Lorrain, Ordinary of Newgate, in the broadsheet relating to an execution at Tyburn on 22 March 1704, describes the proceedings at Tyburn. The ordinary exhorts the criminals to clear their consciences by making a free confession. The malefactors then address the people, praying them to take warning from the example before them. Then the ordinary proceeds to prayer; afterwards to the rehearsal of the articles of the Christian faith, and then comes the singing of penitential hymns, then prayer again. ‘And so, I exhorted them to cry to God for Mercy to the last Moment of their Lives, which they did, and for which they had some time allow’d them. Then the Cart drew away, and they were turn’d off, as they were calling upon God.’

Marks tells us:

In the earliest times the victim, stripped to his shirt, with his arms tied behind his back, was thus dragged along the rough and miry road how rough and iry it is almost impossible for us at this day to realise. That any human being could survive such a drawing from Newgate to Tyburn is marvellous. But the way was not uncommonly longer, from the Tower to Tyburn, or even longer still, from Westminster to the Tower, and then from the Tower to Tyburn. In the case of William Longbeard, it would appear that sharp stones were placed on the road to be followed. But, apart from any such aggravation, the sufferer would probably in most cases be found at the end of the journey incapable of further suffering.

As recorded in the *Annals*, John Price, the Tyburn hangman, was executed in Bunhill-Fields for murder in 1718. In August 1721, John Meff was executed at Tyburn. At a previous date, not mentioned, he had been condemned to death for housebreaking, but, as he was going to Tyburn, the hangman, bearing the generic name of Jack Ketch, was arrested. What became of him is not told, but he probably came to a bad end. In May 1736, Jack Ketch, on his return from doing his office at Tyburn, robbed a woman of 35.6d, for which he was committed to Newgate. History is silent as to his fate. In 1750, the hangman John Thrift was condemned for killing a man in a quarrel. His sentence was commuted to one of transportation for fourteen years. He was finally pardoned, and in September 'resumed the exercise of his office'. In 1780, Edward Dennis, a hangman, was condemned for taking part in the No Popery riots. He was respited. Dickens has introduced Dennis as a personage in his story of *Barnaby Rudge*. It will be seen that, out of the few hangmen of Tyburn whose names have come down to us, several ended their useful lives on the gallows, having failed to profit personally by the lessons they were employed by the state to teach.

2
The Location of the Gallows

There is a plaque on a traffic island near the junction of the Edgware Road and Park Lane claiming to mark the place where the gallows stood. However, there is a question mark as to the exact spot where they stood.

There are a number of sources, dating from the earliest times, that allows us an idea as to not only the nature of the gallows, but where, approximately, they stood. The gallows at Tyburn were permanent until 1759 when, due to the increasing traffic around the area, movable gallows were set up. Marks looked through a large number of early sources with a view to establishing the position of the fixed gallows. The first location he finds 'is in one of the old chronicles, which tells that, in 1330, Mortimer was executed at "The Elms, about a league outside the city". The distance thus vaguely stated would apply about equally to any one of the conjectured sites from Marylebone Lane to the head of the Serpentine, at which writers have severally placed the gallows.'

The *Dickens's Dictionary of London*, 1888, says of the site of the gallows:

> The real site of this spot is a matter of dispute. An iron slab opposite the end of Edgware-rd, and about 50 yards W. of the Marble Arch, professes to designate the precise situation; but No. 49, Connaught-sq, some two or three hundred yards N. W. of that spot, disputes with it the doubtful honour, as does also the portion of the Edgware-rd at the corner of Bryanston-st.

An 1878 history of London makes the following comments as to the exact location of the gallows that 'it would appear, however, to be identified with the site of the house in the south-east corner of Connaught Square, formerly numbered 49; for in the lease granted by the Bishop of London, to whom the property belongs'.

It continues with some interesting eyewitness detail:

This fact is particularly mentioned. A writer in *The Antiquary*, in October, 1873, says, with reference to this subject: 'I was born within 100 yards of the exact spot on which the gallows stood, and my uncle took up the stones on which the uprights were placed'. The following is his statement to me, and the circumstance of his telling it: 'In 1810, when Connaught Place was being built, he was employed on the works, and for many years lived at the corner of Bryanston Street and the Edgware Road, nearly opposite Connaught Mews. My father, a master carpenter, worked for several years in Connaught Place, and on one occasion he employed his brother, I think in the year 1834; at all events, we had just left No. 6, the residence of Sir Charles Coote. It was at this time I said to my uncle, "Now you are here, tell me where the gallows stood;" to which he replied, "Opposite here, where the staves are." I thereupon crossed over, and drove a brass-headed nail into the exact spot he indicated. On reaching home, I told my mother of the occurrence, and asked if it were correct. She said it was so, for she remembered the posts standing when she was a child. This might be about the year 1800; and, as she was born in Bryanston Street, I believe she stated what she knew to be a fact. I well remember Connaught Square being built, and I also recollect a low house standing at the corner of the Uxbridge Road, close to No. 1, Connaught Place (Arklow House), and that, on the removal of this house, quantities of human bones were found. I saw them carted away by Mr Nicholls, contractor, of Adams' Mews. He removed Tyburn toll-house in 1829. From what I have been told by old inhabitants that were born in the neighbourhood, probably about 1750, I have every reason to believe that the space from the toll-house to Frederick Mews was used as a place of execution, and the bodies buried adjacent, for I have seen the remains disinterred when the square and adjoining streets were being built.'

The history continues, referring to additional sources that:

… the gallows were for many years a standing fixture on a small eminence at the corner of the Edgware Road, near the turnpike, on the identical spot where a toll-house was subsequently erected by the Uxbridge Road Trust. Beneath this place are supposed to lie the bones of Bradshaw, Ireton, and other regicides, which were taken from their graves after the Restoration, and buried under the gallows. The gallows itself subsequently consisted of two uprights and a cross-beam, erected on the morning of execution across the Edgware Road, opposite the house at the corner of Upper Bryanston Street and the Edgware Road, wherein the gallows was deposited after being used; this house had curious iron balconies to the windows of the first and second floors, where the sheriffs sat to witness the executions. After the place of execution was changed to Newgate, in 1783, the gallows was bought by a carpenter, and made into stands for beer-butts in the cellars of the 'Carpenters Arms' public-house, hard by. 'Around the gibbet,' says Mr Timbs, in his *Curiosities of London*, 'were erected open galleries, like a race-course stand, wherein seats were let to spectators at executions: the key of one of them was kept by Mammy Douglas, 'the Tyburn pew-opener'. In 1758, when Dr Henesey was to have been executed for treason, the prices of seats rose to 2*s.* and 2*s.* 6*d*; but the doctor being 'most provokingly reprieved,' a riot ensued, and most of the seats were destroyed.

Marks comments that 'we may roughly put its approximate position where the Marble Arch now stands', but he reflects the uncertainty that still remains. It is hard to believe that, as late as the middle of the eighteenth century, Marble Arch and surrounds was rural and sparsely inhabited. The area also lies at the junction of two major Roman roads – Bayswater Road, which becomes Oxford Street, and Watling Street – thus being accessible but suitably remote for a place where gibbets stood containing the bodies of those executed, until the bodies were eaten away or 'waving with the weather while their neck will hold'. This needed to be suitably distant from habitation, but in a place easily seen by travellers as a warning. Thus Tyburn, in its rural location, was eminently suitable.

A further means of pinpointing the site comes when, in 1626, the Catholic wife of Charles I, Henrietta Maria, caused much controversy during a fiercely protestant time by 'going with her attendants through St James's Park to Hyde Park … it was averred that the Queen's confessor had made her walk barefoot to the gallows, "thereby to honour the saint of the day in visiting that holy place, where so many had died"'. Diplomatic rifts with France were avoided by the skill of Marchal de Bassompierre, sent over as Ambassador Extraordinary. Marshal de Bassompierre commented 'that the Queen had not been within fifty paces of the gallows. He repeats the description of the place as at the entrance of a high road.' In conjunction with the antiquary John Norden's (*c.* 1547–1625) map of the area, this can only be the Edgware Road.

1680 John Seller's map of Middlesex shows the gallows near the angle formed by the junction of the roads.

1697 Defoe, in his *Essay upon Projects*, refers to Watling Street: 'The same High Way or Street called Watling Street ... went on West to that spot where Tyburn now stands, and there turn'd North-West ... to St Alban's.'

1725 A large map of the newly constituted parish of St George, Hanover Square, by John Mackay. This shows the first exact location of the gallows, shown as a triangular structure. It is stated that the parish boundary to the west was marked 'on the S.E. Leg of Tyburn', fully proving the permanence of the structure.

1746 Rocque's map of London was published in twenty-four sheets; this was followed by his maps of Middlesex in 1754 and 1757. The gallows are shown in the open space formed by the junction of the roads near the Marble Arch.

1747 In the last plate of Hogarth's series of *Industry and Idleness* is shown an execution at Tyburn. The gallows are in the same position (approximately) as in Rocque's maps.

1756 In Scale's map, the triangular gallows are shown in the same position as in Rocque's maps. Also clear is the development of the area around Tyburn as shown by the inclusion of Tyburn in maps of London. In 1719 it was proposed to move the gallows to Stamford Hill:

> We hear the famous and ancient Engine of Justice called Tyburn is going to be demolished: and we hear the Place of Execution is to be removed to Stamford Hill, beyond Newington, on the way to Ware ... because of the great Buildings that are going to be erected in Maribone-Fields.

In 1759, the permanent gallows gave way to a movable gallows, put up on the day of an execution and afterwards taken down. John Strype (1643–1737), the English Church historian writing in 1720 about Hanover Square, then partly built, says:

> And it is reported that the common Place of Execution of Malefactors at Tyburn, shall be appointed elsewhere, as somewhere near Kingsland; for the removing any Inconveniences or Annoyances, that might thereby be occasioned to that Square, or the Houses thereabouts.

We are told that the removal of the gallows was followed by the occupation of its site by the toll-house of the turnpike, shifted from the east corner of Park Lane, then called Tyburn Lane, to the corner of Edgware Road. The new movable gallows was ordinarily fixed near the corner of Bryanston Street and Edgware Road (Thomas Smith, *A Topographical and Historical Account of the Parish of St. Marylebone*, 1833), but the place of erection was not always exactly the same. Thus we read in *The Gentleman's Magazine* under date 29 August 1783, 'The gallows was fixed about 50 yards nearer the Park wall than usual.'

Due to increasing gentrification of the area, Tyburn ceased to be the place of execution in 1783, the last execution here taking place on 7 November of that year. On removal of the turnpike in 1829, its position was recorded by a slab of cast iron with a gable top with the words on both sides 'HERE STOOD TYBURN GATE 1829'. The monument correctly indicated the position of the gate, which stretched across the road: it was not intended to show the position of the gallows, which, however, it did indicate approximately. The monument was removed in the improvements carried out near the Marble Arch in 1908.

Old and New London, published in 1878, gives us an idea of the nature of the Tyburn district, which at the time was referred to as Tyburnia. We are informed that 'of late years has become almost, if not quite, as fashionable and aristocratic as Belgravia, is the district lying between Edgware Road and Westbourne and Gloucester Terrace and Craven Hill, the south side of which is bounded by the Bayswater Road, and may be said to have sprung into existence only since the reign of William IV'.[7]

The River Tyburn consisted of two branches; one crossed Oxford Street near Stratford Place and the other followed the approximate course of the present Westbourne Terrace and the Serpentine. *Old and New London* paints a picture of a pleasant rural scene where today traffic roars:

> Five hundred years ago, or less, it was a pleasant brook enough, with rows of elms growing on its banks. Elm's Lane, Bayswater, now swept away, preserved down to our own time the memory of these fatal elms, which are to be regarded as the original 'Tyburn Trees.' It was at a subsequent time that the place of execution was removed nearer to London, the corner of the Edgware Road.

The same history tells us that the reason why Tyburn was chosen as the place of execution and burial of traitors was that:

The parishioners of St Sepulchre's, near Newgate, were not over-well pleased that the bodies of those malefactors who had suffered the last penalty of the law should be buried amongst them; in proof, it may be mentioned, on the authority of a letter from Fleetwood to Lord Burghley, that they 'would not suffer a traytor's corpes to be layed in the earthe where theire parents, wyeffs, chyldren, kynred, maisters, and old naighboures did rest: and so his carcas was returned to the buryall ground neere to Tyborne'.

3

Annals of the Condemned

The history *Tyburn Tree, Its History and Annals,*[8] by Alfred Marks, looks at extensive records relating to those that were executed at Tyburn from earliest times. The research is extensive, but in style it is long-winded and often strays into moral discourses on man's inhumanity to man. I have used much of Marks' source material, but have edited it to make it readable in both modern and ancient language, where used, and highlight the key points of interest. The quoting of original sources does much to convey the attitudes and feeling of the times relating to the dealing out of what was frequently barbaric punishment. As this chapter relies largely on extant sources, my input will be presented in italics.

1177 The first recorded execution which can be referred to Tyburn occurred in this year. It is probable that Tyburn was the place of execution, but, leaving this case aside for the time, we come to the execution of William Fitz Osbert, or Longbeard, expressly stated to have been carried out at Tyburn.

1196 William Fitz Osbert, or Osborn, popularly known as Longbeard, was a citizen of London, described as skilled in the law. He is first made known to us by the story of a vision seen by him and a companion on board a ship, one of the fleet of Richard Coeur de Lion (Richard I), on its way to the Holy Land. In a great storm at sea there appeared to them three times St Thomas of Canterbury, who said to them, 'Fear not, for I and the Blessed Martyr Edmund, and the Blessed Confessor Nicholas have taken charge of this ship of the King of England. And if the men of this ship will eschew evil and seek pardon for past offences, God will give them a prosperous voyage.' Having thrice said this, he vanished and the storm ceased. This was in 1190. Richard, on his return, was captured and held to ransom by the emperor. The raising of the ransom proved very grievous to the people. There was trouble in the City of London as to the way of assessing the burden. The poorer sort claimed that the citizens should not be called on to pay so much per head, whether rich or poor, but that the assessment should be according to means. William Longbeard took the part of the poor citizens: it came to be a matter to be fought to the death between the magnates and Longbeard. Moreover, Longbeard had accused of extortion Hubert, Archbishop of Canterbury and Justiciar. An armed band was told off to arrest Longbeard. He resisted, slew two chiefs of the band, but was compelled to fly for protection to the church of St Mary-le-Bow. [*The church still stands in Cheapside*]. Then the archbishop did a thing unheard of. He, a churchman, bound by every consideration to guard the privileges of the church, set at nought the right of sanctuary, kindled a fire, and drove Longbeard out of the church. In his attempt to escape Longbeard was wounded by the son of one of those whom he had killed in trying to escape arrest. He was hurried to trial: the great men of the city and the king's officers joined in urging the justiciar to inflict the severest punishment on the offender. This was the punishment: his upper garments were taken off, then his hands were bound behind his back, and, attached by ropes to a horse, he was dragged from the Tower through the City to Tyburn, and there hanged alive by a chain. What was he, unscrupulous demagogue or martyr in the cause of the poor? Each view was held by his contemporaries. He seems to have behaved very badly to his elder brother, whose care for him during his youth he repaid by bringing against him a charge of treason. On the other hand, it is clear that Longbeard's enemies had against him a case which it was necessary to strengthen by baseless accusations. He was charged with blaspheming the Virgin Mary, and with taking his concubine into Bow Church. The last charge seems disproved by the circumstances in which Longbeard fled to the church for refuge. It was also set about that he was put to death for 'heresy and cursed doctrine' whereas it is obvious that his offence was political. Be this as it may, his enemies triumphed; Longbeard was drawn and hanged with nine of his fellows. But 'the simple people honoured him as a Martyre, insomuch that they steale away the gibbet whereon he was hanged, & pared away the earth, that was be-bled with his blood, and kept the same as holy reliques to heale si eke men'. Hubert, the archbishop, drove them away. But two years later the monks of Canterbury presented to the Pope charges against Hubert. The first is that he had violated the peace of the Church of Bow by forcing out Longbeard and his fellows. The Pope advised Richard to remove Hubert from the office of justiciar, and not to employ churchmen in secular offices. Hubert resisted for a while, but in the end accepted his dismissal. Stow, in his *Survey* says that Longbeard was hanged at 'the Elms in Smithfield', but there is no authority for this. We find mention of an execution of a date earlier than that of Longbeard, taking place at London, for a crime of which the royal court would necessarily have cognisance, it is at least highly probable that Tyburn, though not expressly mentioned, was the place of execution. The crime of 1177 is one of those few social crimes, as distinguished from political offences, of which the chroniclers make mention; the story reveals a strange picture of the manners of the time. During a council held at London the brother of the Earl Ferrers was murdered in his inn, the body being afterwards thrown into the mud of the street. When the king heard of this he was greatly moved, and swore that he would visit the crime heavily upon the citizens of London. For it was said that a hundred and more of the sons and relatives of the nobles of the City were in the habit of breaking into the houses of wealthy men for the purpose of robbery. And if they found any one going by night about the streets they forthwith murdered him without pity, so that for fear of them few dared to go about the City by night. So it came about that in the third year before this, the sons and nephews of certain nobles of the City, meeting together by night, for the sake of plunder broke into the stone house of a certain rich man of London, using iron wedges for the purpose of making an opening, by which they entered. But the head of the house had been warned beforehand of their intent, wherefore he put on a leather cuirass, and had with him several nobles and trusty servants also protected by armour, sitting with him in a corner of the house. And when he saw one of those thieves, by name Andrew Bucquinte, pressing on in front of the others with glowing face, he brought forward a pot full of live coals, and hurriedly kindled some wax tapers which he carried in his hand, and rushed upon him. Which beholding, the said Andrew

Bucquinte drew his knife from its sheath and struck the master of the house; but he failed to wound him because the blow fell upon the cuirass. And the master of the house quickly drawing his sword from its sheath, returned the blow, and lopped off the right hand of the said Andrew Bucquinte, crying with a loud voice, 'Thieves, thieves!' and hearing this all fled except him who had lost his hand, he being held by the master of the house. And when day broke he took him to Richard de Lucy, the king's justice, who threw him into prison. And the thief, on promise of life and limb, gave up the names of his companions, many of whom were taken, though many also escaped. Among those taken was a certain very noble and very rich citizen of London, by name John Senex, who being unable to clear himself by the ordeal of water, offered to the king five hundred marks of silver for his life. But as he was condemned by the ordeal of water, the king refused to accept the money, and ordered that judgment should be done upon him, and he was hanged.

1221 In this year Constantine Fitz-Athulf was hanged, and that without trial. The story of the execution without trial of one who had been sheriff of the great and powerful City compels attention. It is thus told by the chroniclers, the date assigned being 1222 or 1223: In this year, on the feast of St James the Apostle,[9] the inhabitants of London and those of the neighbouring country, having challenged one another to a wrestling match, met near the hospital of Queen Matilda, outside the City [*St Katherine's Hospital, near the Tower. St Katherine's Marina now stands on the site*] to decide who were the stronger in this sport. The contest was long, and after great efforts on both sides, the citizens of London had the best of the contest, to the chagrin of their adversaries. He who took the defeat most to heart was the seneschal of the abbat of Westminster, who devised means to avenge the defeat of his party. Having formed in his mind a plan of vengeance, he issued a fresh challenge for the feast of St Peter's Chains [1 August], and sent word for everyone to come to Westminster to wrestle, promising a ram as a prize. That being done the said seneschal got together strong and practised wrestlers, so that the victory might be thus gained. The citizens of London, wishing to distinguish themselves a second time, came in great numbers to the appointed place. The contest began, those on one side and the other trying to throw their opponents to the ground, but the seneschal of whom mention has been made, having brought up people from the neighbourhood and from the country, turned the contest into a fight which would satisfy his revenge. He took up arms without provocation and furiously charged, not without bloodshed, the unarmed citizens. The citizens, wounded and insulted, fled in disorder to the City. There ensued a great tumult: the common bell was rung and brought the people together. The story went about, every one gave his opinion, and proposed his plan of revenge. At last the Mayor, Serle, a man prudent and peaceful, advised that complaint should be made to the abbat of Westminster, and said that if he would consent to make suitable reparation, every one should then be satisfied. But Constantine, who had great power in the City, declared amid great applause that it would be better to throw down all the houses belonging to the abbat of Westminster, as well as the seneschal's house. Forthwith an order was drawn up, enjoining the immediate execution of Constantine's project. A blind multitude, a mad populace, entrusted Constantine with this civil war, flung itself in a tumult on the possessions of the abbat, demolished several houses, and did great damage. In the midst of this scene was Constantine, continually reciting the order, and crying with all his might, 'Montjoie! Montjoi! God and our lord Louis be our help!' This cry, more than anything else, provoked the king's friends, and made them determine to exact punishment for this sedition, as we will now tell. The facts soon got about, and came to the ear of Hubert de Burgh, the justiciar, who, having got together a number of knights, put himself at their head and went to the Tower of London, from which he sent a message to the elders to come to him without delay. When they were before him he asked who were the principal movers in the sedition; who were they who had dared to trouble the royal city, and break the king's peace? Then Constantine, constant in his presumption and pride, answered otherwise than was either becoming or prudent. 'It is I,' he said, 'what wilt thou?' He declared that he was protected by treaty, that he could justify what he had done, which was even less than he ought to have done. He trusted to the oath taken by the king as well as by Prince Louis, by the terms of which the friends and partisans of one or the other were to be left in peace. The justiciar, hearing this avowal of Constantine, detained him and two of his abettors, without exciting any disturbance. The next morning he sent Fawkes de Breaute (known to him as a man ready for any cruelty) with an armed force to carry Constantine by way of the Thames to be hanged at The Elms. Quickly and secretly they carried him thither, and when Constantine had the rope round his neck, he offered fifteen thousand marks silver if his life might be spared. To whom answer was made that never more should he get up a riot in the king's city. Hanged therefore he was, together with Constantine, his nephew, and a certain Geoffrey, who had proclaimed the order in the City. Thus was the sentence on Constantine carried out unknown to the citizens, and without disorder. That done, the justiciar made his entry into London, with Fawkes and the armed men who had gone with him. He arrested all known to have taken part in the riot, threw them into prison, and let them out only when he had caused their feet or hands to be lopped off. Numbers fled and never returned. The king took sixty citizens as hostages, and deposed the magistrates and put others in their room. Moreover, he ordered that a great gallows should be set up.

1236 About this time some bold but rash nobles in England, seduced by we know not what spirit, conspired together, and entered into an execrable alliance to ravage England like robbers and night-thieves. Their design, however, became known, and the chief of the conspiracy to wit, Peter de Buffer, one of the king's doorkeepers was taken prisoner, and by him others were accused. In order to whose execution a dreadful machine, commonly called a gibbet, was set up in London, and on it two of the chief conspirators were hanged, after having engaged in single combat. One of them was killed in the fight, and was hanged with his head cleft open, and the other, hanged alive, breathed forth his wretched life on the same gibbet amid the lamentations of the assembled multitude.

1239 A certain messenger of the king, named William, had been convicted of manifold crimes, and lay in prison under sentence of death. He brought accusations of treason against several nobles; he also made a criminal charge against Ralph Briton, a priest and canon of the Church of St Paul's, London, who had for some time been a familiar friend of the king, and had held the office of treasurer. On this coming to the king's ears he by letter ordered the Mayor of London, William Gromer (or Gerard Batt), to seize Ralph and imprison him in the Tower of London, and the Mayor obeying the king rather than God, at once carried the king's orders into effect. He dragged the said Ralph with violence from his house near St Paul's, and imprisoned him in the Tower, securing him with chains, commonly called rings. The Dean of London, Master G. de Lucy, informed of this, took counsel with his fellow canons (the bishop being absent), and pronounced a general sentence of excommunication against all the presumptuous perpetrators of this enormity, and placed St Paul's Church under an interdict. The king, however, although warned by the bishop, did not amend his faults, but continued with threats to heap evils on evils, so that the bishop was about to place the whole of the City of London, which was subject to him, under an interdict : but when the archbishop of Canterbury, as well as the legate, the bishop of London, and many other prelates, were prepared to lay a heavy hand on the City, the king, although unwillingly, ordered the said Ralph to be released, and allowed to depart in peace. But when the king sought to add the condition that Ralph should be so kept as to be ready to give an explanation when the king required it, the churchmen replied that they would not on any account keep him in this manner, like an imprisoned man, but that the church should receive him as absolutely free, just as when the king's attendants tore him by force from his house. In this manner then was Ralph released. Not long afterwards, the before-named villain, who had, as above stated, calumniated the nobles and the aforesaid Ralph, was ignominiously hanged outside the City of London, on that instrument of punishment called a gibbet: and when he saw that death was certain, he, although late, openly confessed before the people and his executioners that he had made the aforesaid accusations only for the purpose of prolonging his life.

1278 In the month of November in this year all Jews throughout England were seized on the same day, imprisoned in London, for clipping the king's coin. And the Jews gave information as to very many Christians in league with them, and chiefly among the more renowned of London. On this occasion two hundred and eighty Jews of both sexes were hanged at London: in other cities of England a very great multitude. The king exacted an immense sum for the ransom of the Christians, some of whom also were delivered to the gallows.

1284 In this year Bow church witnessed a great tragedy. In 1196 it was the scene of a terrible affair. It may be told mainly in the words of the historian Stow (1597): 'In the year 1284, the 13th of Edward I, Laurence Ducket, goldsmith, having grievously wounded one Ralph Crepin in Westcheape, fled into Bow church, into the which, in the night time, entered certain evil persons, friends unto the said Ralph, and slew the said Laurence, lying in the steeple, and then hanged him up, placing him so by the window as if he had hanged himself, and so was it found by inquisition: for the which fact Laurence Ducket, being drawn by the feet, was buried in a ditch without the City: (suicides were not allowed to be buried in consecrated ground) but shortly after, by relation of a boy, who lay with the said Laurence at the time of his death, and had hid himself there for fear, the truth of the matter was disclosed. Wherefore a certain woman, Alice atte Bowe, the mistress of Crepin, a clerk, the chief causer of the said mischief, and with her sixteen men, were imprisoned, and later, Alice was burnt, and seven were drawn and hanged, to wit, Reginald de Lanfar, Robert Pinnot, Paul de Stybbenheth, Thomas Corouner, John de Tholosane, Thomas Russel, and Robert Scott. Ralph Crepin, Jordan Godchep, Gilbert le Clerk and Geoffrey le Clerk were attainted of the felony and remained prisoners in the Tower. The church was placed under an interdict by the archbishop: the doors and windows stopped up with thorns. But the body of Laurence was taken from the place where it lay, and given burial by the clergy in the churchyard. After a while, the bishop of Rochester, by command of the archbishop, removed the interdict.'

1295 October 6. The Treason of Sir Thomas Turberville. Sir Thomas Turberville, taken prisoner by the French, was released in order that he might return to England and act as a secret agent for the French government. He was detected in corresponding with the Provost of Paris, tried and condemned. This was the manner of his execution: he came from the Tower, mounted on a poor hack, in a coat of ray, and shod with white shoes, his head being covered with a hood, and his feet tied beneath the horse's belly, and his hands tied before him and around him were riding six torturers attired in the form of the devil, one of whom held his rein, and the hangman his halter, for the horse which bore him had them both upon it: and in such manner was he led from the Tower through London to

Westminster, and was condemned on the dais in the Great Hall there: and Sir Robert Brabazun pronounced judgment upon him, that he should be drawn and hanged, and that he should hang so long as anything should be left whole of him: and he was drawn on a fresh ox-hide from Westminster to the Conduit of London in Cheapside, and then back to the gallows and there is he hung by a chain of iron, and will hang as long as anything of him may remain. The place of execution is not mentioned. The probability is all in favour of the Elms of Tyburn.

1305 August 23 William Wallace (Braveheart) drawn from Westminster to the Tower and thence to Tyburn, where he was hanged and quartered. In treating of the punishment for high treason, mention has already been made of the manner of carrying out the sentence on Wallace, 'the man of Belial', as he is constantly called in the Chronicles. Wallace was hanged on a very high gallows, specially made for the occasion. Edward was fond of high gallows. At the siege of Stirling Castle, in 1300, he caused to be erected two gallows, sixty feet high, before the gates of the castle, and swore a great oath (*jurra graunt serment*) that if surrender was not at once made, he would hang every one within the castle, were he earl, baron, or knight, high or low. 'On hearing which,' says the chronicler, 'those within at once opened the gates and surrendered to the king, who pardoned them.' The place of execution of Wallace was undoubtedly Tyburn. 'The Elms' is mentioned in Chronicles of the reigns of Edward I and Edward II, The sentence bore that Wallace's head should be exposed on London Bridge. This is the first recorded instance of a head being exposed here.[10]

1306 Two other executions of Scottish leaders followed, both probably at Tyburn, though the place is not expressly mentioned. Symon Frisel [Fraser] was brought to London, and then, according to the chronicler, drawn, on 7 September, from the Tower, through the streets to the gallows as traitor, hanged as thief, beheaded as murderer; then his body was hung on a gibbet for twenty days, and finally burnt, the head placed on London Bridge. The execution of the earl of Athol followed on 7 November. Edward, grievously ill, found his pains relieved by learning of the capture of the earl. Athol claimed to be of royal lineage. 'If he is of nobler blood than the other parricides,' said Edward, 'he shall be hanged higher than they.' He was carried to London, and condemned at Westminster. Then, as being of royal descent, he was not drawn, but rode on horseback to the place of execution, where he was hanged on a gallows fifty feet high. Then let down, half alive, so that his torment might be greater, very cruelly beheaded (the chronicler does not say what was done to make the beheading unusually cruel), then the body was thrown into a fire previously kindled in the sight of the sufferer, and reduced to ashes. Then the head was placed on London Bridge among those of other traitors, but higher than the rest, in regard to his royal descent.

1307 In May, John Wallace was brought to London, condemned as a traitor and hanged. His head was set on London Bridge near that of William Wallace.

1330 Edward III was but a boy when crowned in February, 1327. All power was in the hands of Isabella, his mother, queen of the deposed and murdered king, Edward II, and of her lover, Roger Mortimer, baron of Wigmore and earl of March. For the murder of Edward II the queen-mother and Mortimer are held to be specially responsible. In 1329 a powerful confederation was formed to overthrow Mortimer. This was for the time defeated, but Edward, now eighteen, chafed under his subjection and took counsel with William de Montacute. It was resolved to seize Mortimer in the castle of Nottingham, where, during the session of Parliament held there, Isabella and her lover lodged. Mortimer was well guarded, and it was necessary to bring into the confederation Sir William Eland, the governor of the castle. He told the confederates of a subterranean passage, unknown to Mortimer, and unwatched, through which a sufficient force could be introduced. The rest of the story may be told in the words of Stow: 'Then, upon a certaine night, the King lying without the castle, both he and his friends were brought by torch light through a secret way vnder ground, beginning far off from the sayde castle, till they came even to the Queenes chamber, which they by chance found open: they therefore being armed with naked swords in their hands, went forwards, leaving the King also armed with-out the doore of the Chamber, least that his mother shoulde espie him: they which entred in, slew Hugh Turpinton knight, who resisted them, Master John Nevell of Home by giving him his deadly wound. From thence, they went towarde the Queene mother, whom they found with the Earle of March readie to have gone to bedde: and having taken the sayde Earle, they ledde him out into the hall, after whom the Queene followed, crying, Belfilz, belfilz, ayes pitie de gentil Mortimer, Good sonne, good sonne, take pittie upon gentle Mortimer: for she suspected that her sonne was there, though shee saw him not. Then are the Keyes of the Castle sent for, and every place with all the furniture is yeelded up into the kings handes, but in such secret wise, that none without the Castle, except the kinges friendes, understoode thereof. The next day in the morning verie early, they bring Roger Mortimer, and other his friends taken with him, with an horrible shout and crying (the earle of Lancaster then blind, being one of them that made the showt for joy) towardes London, where hee was committed to the Tower, and afterward condemned at Westminster, in presence of the whole Parliament on Saynt Andrewes even next following, and then drawne to the Elmes and there hanged on the common Gallowes. Whereon hee hung two dayes and two nights by the kings commaundement, and then was buryed in the Gray Fryars Church.' (*The ruins of Grey Friars still remain*). It has been frequently said that Mortimer was the first person executed at Tyburn. The *French Chronicle of London* says, 'Sir Roger Mortimer, and Sir Symon de Bereford, who was of his counsel, were drawn and hanged at London.'

In a note Mr Riley adds that he 'is said to have been the first person executed at Tyburn, but according to Roger of Wendover, William Fitz-Osbert, or Longbeard, was executed there in 1196'. Dr Lingard says that Mortimer 'was executed at Tyburn, the first, as it is said, who honoured with his death that celebrated spot'. The reader now knows that not only Longbeard, but Constantine Fitz-Athulf, had certainly been here executed, and also probably others mentioned in these Annals. It may be taken for granted that the new gallows erected in 1220, and the old gallows replaced by them, had not stood idle. In the century-and-a-half during which the gallows had stood at Tyburn, hundreds, if not thousands of unrecorded executions must have taken place here.

1347 The Scotch king, David II, the Earl of Fife, and the Earl of Menteith were captured. Fife and Menteith were sent to London and tried. From Calais Edward III sent the judgment to be pronounced on these two 'traitors and tyrants'. In accordance with the sentence,

Menteith was drawn, hanged, disembowelled. His head was set on
London Bridge, and the quarters sent to various parts of England.
The sentence was not carried out against Fife, as being allied to the
king in blood.

1377 Sir John Menstreworth, accused of embezzling from the king
large sums allotted to him for the pay of soldiers, fled to France.
About this time (April), writes the chronicler, was captured Sir John
Menstreworth, a traitorous knight, who had fled to Pamplona, a city
of Navarre. Brought to London, he was first drawn, then hanged:
finally his body was divided into four quarters, which were sent to
four principal cities of England; and his head was fixed on London
Bridge, where it remained for a long time.

1386 'And that yere the goode man at the sygne at the Cocke in
Chepe, at the Lyttyll Condyte, was mortheryd in hys bedde be nyght,
and therefore hys wyffe was brente, and iiij of hys men were hangyd
at Tyborne.' The *Grey Friars Chronicle* says that three servants were
drawn and hanged. This is the record of a terrible judicial error. The
Chronicles tell the story, some under the year 1386, some under
1391. We may suppose that the dates are those respectively of the
commission of the crime and the discovery of the real criminal. Stow
in 1598 thus tells the whole story: 'the good man of the Cocke in
Cheap at the little conduit was murdered in the night time by a thiefe
that came in at a gutter window, as it was knowne long after by the
same thiefe, when he was at the gallowes to be hanged for felonie,
but his wife was burnt therefore, and three of his men drawne to
Tiburne, and there hanged wrongfully.' One of the old chroniclers,
after telling the story, adds, 'and that was truth'. What more can be
said in presence of such a calamity?

1388 The struggle for power under the rule of the boy-king,
Richard I, ended in the utter rout of one of the two factions. This
is Stow's narrative: 'The foresaid Lords being fled as is aforesaide,
Robert Trisilian a Cornishman, Lord chiefe Justice to the King, had
hid himselfe in an Apothecaries house in the Sanctuary neere to
the gate of Westminster, where he might see the Lords going to the
Parliament, and comming forth thereby to learne what was done,
for all his life time he did all things closely, but now his craft being
espied was turned to great folly. For on Wednesday the seventeenth
of February he was betraied of his owne servant, & about eleven of

the clocke before noone, being taken by the Duke of Glocester, and in the Parliament presented, so that the same day in the after noone hee was drawne to Tyborne from the Tower of London through the Citie, & there had his throat cut and his bodie was buried in the gray Friers Church at London. This man had disfigured himselfe, as if he had beene a poore weake man, in a frize coat, all old & torne, and had artificially made himselfe a long beard, such as they called a Paris beard, and had defiled his face, to the end hee might not bee knowen but by his speach. On the morrow, was executed sir Nicholas Brembar, who had done many oppressions, & caused seditions in the Citie, of whom it was saide, y whilest he was in full authoritie of Majoralitie, hee caused a common payre of Stockes in every ward, and a common Axe to be made to behead all such as should bee against him, and it was further said, that hee had indited 8000. & more of the best and greatest of the Citie, but it was said that the said Nicholas was beheaded with the same Axe hee hadde prepared for other: this man if hee hadde lived, hadde beene created Duke of Troy, or of London by the name of Troy. On the fourth of March Thomas Uske, Undershrive (*under-sherrif*) of London, & Iohn Blake Esquire, one of the kings household, were drawne from the Tower to Tyborne and there hanged and beheaded, the head of Thomas Uske was set up over Newgate, to the opprobry of his parents, which inhabited thereby. Also on the 12 of May ... Sir John Bernes knight of the kings Court ... was in the same place [Tower hill] beheaded, sir John Salisburie knight was drawne from the Tower to Tyborne and there hanged.' Some of the accounts state that Brembre was hanged at Tyburn, but Knighton says that he was beheaded on Tower Hill, the king having stipulated with Parliament that he should not be drawn nor hanged. Walsingham says that Little Troy was the new name intended to be given by Brembre to London.[11]

1399 In this year took place several executions for the murder of the Duke of Gloucester at Calais. John Hall was charged with having kept the door of the room when the Duke was done to death by being smothered in a feather-bed... 'the lordes were examyned what peyne the same John Halle hadde desyrved ffor his knowyng off the deeth off the Duk off Gloucestre: and the lordes seyden, that he were worthy the moste grete peyne and penaunce that he myght have. And so the Juggement was that the same John Halle shulde be drawe from the Tour off London to Tyborne, and ther his bowelles shulde be brent (*burnt*) and affterwarde he shulde be hangid and quarterid and byhedid. And his heede brouht to the same place, wher the Duk off Gloucestre was murdred.'

1400 After the deposition of Richard II and the coronation of Henry IV a conspiracy was formed to surprise Henry at a tournament to be held at Windsor in December, 1399. The plot was made known by the Earl of Rutland, one of the conspirators. Henry collected an army in London, and set out for the rebels' camp near Windsor. The rebels retreated to Cirencester, where they were overthrown. According to the *Chronicle of London* (1827), Sir Thomas Blount, Sir Bennet Shelley, Thomas Wyntreshull, and about twenty-seven others, were executed at Oxford. 'Afterwards was taken Sr. Bernard Brocas, Sr. Thomas Schelley, Maudelyn parson, Sr. William Fereby prest: and there were drawen, hanged, and beheded at Tyborne.'

1404 The olde Countesse of Oxford, mother to Robert de Vere Duke of Ireland did cause such as were familiar with her, to brute throughout all the parts of Essex, that king Richard was alive, and that he should shortely come & chalenge his olde estate and dignitie. She caused many harts of silver, and some of golde to be made for badges, such as king Richard was wont to bestowe on his knights, Esquiers & friends, that distributing them in the kings name, she might the sooner allure the knights, and other valiant men of the Countrey, to be at her will and desire. Also the fame and brute which daily was blazed abroad by one William Serle, sometimes of K.Richards chamber, that the same King Richard was in Scotland, and tarryed with a power of French & Scottishmen, caused many to beleeve that he was alive. This William Serle had forged a privie Seale in the said Richards name, and had sent divers comfortable letters unto such as were familiar with K. Richard, by which meanes, many gave the greater credit to the Countesse, insomuch, that some religious Abbots of that country did give credit unto her tales who afterward were taken at the Kings commaundement and imprisoned, because they did beleeve and give credit to the Countesse in this behalfe, and the Countesse had all her goods confiscate, and was committed to close prison: and William Serle, was drawn from pomfret, through the chiefest Citties of England, and put to death at London.' *Gregory's Chronicle* supplies the place of execution Tyburn.

1424 The Parliament sitting in this year 'ordained that what prysoner for grand or petty treason was committed to ward, & after wilfully brake or made an escape from the same, it should bee deemed pettie treason.' Sir John Mortimer lay in the Tower, accused of diver points of treason. 'Which John Mortimer, after the statute aforesaid escaped out of the tower, and was taken againe upon the tower wharfe sore beaten and wounded, and on the morrowe brought to Westminster, and by the authoritie of the said parliament, hee was drawne to Tyburne, hanged & headed.'[12]

1446 John David appeached his master William Catur, an armorer dwelling in S. Dunstons parish in Fleetstreet, of treason, & a day being assigned them to fight in Smithfield, ye master being welbeloved, was so cherished by his friends & plied so with wine, that being therwith overcome was also unluckely slaine by his servant: but that false servant (for he falsely accused his master) lived not long unpunished, for he was after hanged at Tyborne for felony.[13]

1447 And anon aftyr the dethe of the Duke of Glouceter there were a reste [arrested] many of the sayde dukys [servants] to the nombyr of 38 squyers, be-syde alle othyr servantys that nevyr ymagenyd no falsenys of [that] they were put apon of. And on Fryday the 14 day of Juylle nexte folowynge by jugement at Westemyster, there by fore 5 personys were deemed to be drawe, hanggyd, and hyr bowellys i-brente b fore them, and thenne thyr heddys to be smetyn of, ande thenne to be quarteryde, and every parte to be sende unto dyvers placys by assygnement of the judgys. Whyche personys were thes: Arteys the bastarde of the sayde Duke of Glouceter, Syr Rogger Chambyrlayne knyght, Mylton squyer, Thomas Harberde squyer, Nedam yeman, whyche were the sayde 14 day of Juylle drawen from St Gofgys thoroughe owte Sowthewerke and on Londyn Brygge, ande so forthe thorowe the cytte of London to the Tyborne, and there alle they were hanggyde, and the ropys smetyn asondyr, they beynge alle lyvynge, and thenne, ar any more of any markys of excecusyon were done, the Duke of Sowthefolke (Suffolk) brought them alle yn generalle pardon and grace from our lorde and soverayne Kynge Harry the vi.

1495 The 22. of Februarie were arraigned in Guildhall at London foure persons, to witte, Thomas Bagnall, John Scot, John Hethe, and John Kenington, the which were Sanctuarie men of Saint Martin le grand in London, and lately before taken thence, for forging seditious libels, to the slander of the King, and some of his Councell: for the which three of them were adjudged to die, & the fourth named Bagnall, pleaded to be restored to sanctuary: by reason whereof he was reprived to the Tower till the next terme.[14]

1495 In this year Perkin Warbeck, a pretender, 'A yoongman, of visage beautifull, of countenance demure, of wit subtil', made a descent on the English coasts: 'But Perken would not set one foote out of his Shippe, till he sawe all thinges sure; yet he permitted some of his Souldiours to goe on lande, which being trained forth a prettie way from their Shippes, and seeing they coulde have no comfort of the Countrey, they withdrew againe to their Shippes: at which withdrawing, the Major of Sandwich, with certaine commons of the Countrey, bickered with the residue that were uppon lande, and tooke alive of them 169 persons, among the which were five Captaines Mountfort, Corbet, White Belt, Quintin & Genine. And on the twelfth of Julie, Syr John Pechy, Sheriffe of Kent, bought unto London bridge those 169. persons, where the Sheriffes of London, Nicholas Alwine and John Warner received and conveied them, railed in robes like horses in a cart, unto the tower of London, and to Newgate, and shortlie after to the number of 150 were hanged about the sea coasts in Kent, Essex, Sussex, and Norffolk; the residue were executed at Tiborne and at Wapping ... and Perken fled into Flanders.'[15]

1499 Perkyn (of whome rehersall was made before) beyng now in holde, coulde not leave with the destruccion of him selfe, and confusion of other that had associate them selfes with him, but began now to study which way to flye & escape. For he by false persuasions and liberall promises corrupted Strangweyes, Blewet, Astwood and Jon Rogier hys kepers, beynge servantes to sir John Dygby, lieutenaunt. In so muche that they (as it was at their araynment openly proved) entended to have slayn the sayde Master, and to have set Perkyn and the Erle of Warwyke at large; which Earle was by them made privy of this enterprice, & thereunto (as all naturall creatures love libertie) to his destruccion assented. But this craftie device and subtil imagination, beyng opened and disclosed, sorted to none effect, and so he beyng repulsed and put back from all hope and good lucke with all hys complices and confederates, and John Awater sometyme

Mayre of Corffe in Ireland, one of his founders, and his sonne, were the sixteen daye of Novembre arreyned and comdemned at Westmynster. And on the three and twenty daye of the same moneth, Perkyn and John Awater were drawen to Tyborne, and there Perkyn standyng on a little skaffolde, read hys confession, which before you have heard, and toke it on hys death to be true, and so he and John Awater asked the kyng forgevenes and dyed paciently.[16]

1502 Upon Monday, beyng the second day of May, was kept at the Guyld hall of London an hour determyne, where sat the Mayre, the Duke of Bokyngham, The earle of Oxford, with many other lordes, Judges, and knyghtes, as commyssioners: before whome was presented as prisoners to be enquyred of, sir James Tyrell, and sir John Wyndam, knyghtes, a Gentilman of the said sir James, named Wellesbourn, and one other beyng a shipman … Upon friday folowyng, beyng the 6th day of May and the morowe after the Ascension of our Lord, Sir James Tyrell and the forsaid Sir John Wyndam, knyghtes, were brought out of the Towre to the scaffold upon the Towre hill, upon their feete, where they were both beheded. And the same day was the forsaid Shipman laied upon an hurdyll, and so drawen from the Towre to Tybourne, and there hanged, hedid, and quartered. And the forenamed Wellysbourn Remayned still in prison at the kynges commandment and pleasure.[17]

1523 About eight miles from Bath is a village, Farleigh-Hungerford, known locally as Farleigh Castle from the extensive ruins of what was once a proud castle full of life and movement. As the name denotes, the Castle was the seat one of the seats of the Hungerford family, established at Heytesbury so far back as the twelfth century. In 1369 the Hungerford of his day, Sir Thomas Hungerford, purchased the manor of Farleigh. In 1383 he obtained permission to convert the manor-house into a castle. Sir Thomas made a great figure in the world: he is the first person formally mentioned in the rolls of Parliament as holding the office of Speaker. Marks, writing in 1908 continues: Wandering among the vast ruins, the visitor, prompted by his guide-book, will not fail to note the spot where was formerly a furnace. If there is in all England a place where ghosts should walk, where the midnight owl should hoot, it is in the ruins of Farleigh Castle. For, now nearly four hundred years ago, Farleigh Castle was the scene of a terrible crime, expiated, perhaps in part only, by the death on the scaffold of one of the principal criminals, and of one or two of the abettors of an over-reaching ambition, or of a lawless passion. In the *Chronicle of the Grey Friars* is the following passage: '1523. And this yere in February the 20th day was the lady Alys Hungerford was lede from the Tower unto Holborne, and there put in-to a carte at the church- yerde with one of her servanttes, and so carred unto Tyborne, and there bothe hangyd, and she burryd at the Grayfreeres in the nether end of the myddes of the churche on the northe syde.' Stow adds a particular omitted by the earlier Chronicler that the lady was executed for the murder of her husband. *Marks tells us that the curiosity of antiquaries was naturally excited by this story, half-revealed, half-concealed.* The first discovery made was of the inventory of the lady's goods. This was printed in *Archaeologia, vol. xxxviii* (1860). The goods fell into the hands of the king by forfeiture: so it came about that an inventory existed. It is a list of plate and jewels, of sumptuous hangings, 'an extraordinary collection of valuable property'. Finally more of the story was disclosed by Mr William John Hardy, in the *Antiquary* of December, 1880. It is one of the greatest interest. The lady's name is given as Alice, both by the chronicler and by Stow in his *Annals*. Stow also, in a list of the monuments in the Grey Friars church, mentions one to 'Alice Lat Hungerford, hanged at Tiborne for murdering her husband'. But the lady's name was not Alice, but Agnes. She was the second wife of Sir Edward Hungerford, who was first married to Jane, daughter of John Lord Zouche of Haryngworth. The date of the death of Sir Edward's first wife is not known. If we knew it there might arise a new suspicion. Nor do we know the date of Sir Edward's second marriage, but it must have been not earlier than the latter half of 1518. Sir Edward Hungerford was one of the great ones of the land. In 1517 he was sheriff for Wilts: in 1518 for Somerset and Dorset. In 1520 he was present at the Field of the Cloth of Gold. In 1521 he was in Commission of the Peace for Somerset. We have seen that the original seat of the family was at Heytesbury, in Wilts, distance from Farleigh about twelve miles, and here Sir Edward commonly lived. In addition to Farleigh Castle, Sir Edward possessed a great London house, standing with its gardens where now is Charing Cross station. From this house were named Hungerford Street and Hungerford Stairs. On the site of the house and garden was built by a later Hungerford, in the reign of Charles II, Hungerford Market, which continued till the site was taken for the railway station. The foot-bridge over the Thames, starting from this point, was known as Hungerford Bridge, a name still sometimes given to its successor, the existing railway bridge. It was in Hungerford Street that Charles Dickens, a child of ten, began life by sticking labels on blacking bottles. Sir Edward made his will on 14 December 1521. By it, after leaving legacies to certain churches and friends, 'the residue of all my goods, debts, cattails, juells, plate, harnesse, and all other moveables whatsoever they be, I freely geve and bequeth to Agnes Hungerforde my wife'. She was also appointed sole executrix. Sir Edward died on 24 January 1522, six weeks after making this will. The husband murdered was not Sir Edward Hungerford, but a first husband, John Cotell. The outlines of the story are given by Mr Hardy from the Coram Kege Roll for Michaelmas term, 14 Henry VIII: 'On the Monday next after the feast of S. Bartholomew, in the 14th year of the now king (25 August 1522), at Ilchester, before John Fitz James and his fellow- justices of oyer and terminer for the county of Somerset, William Mathewe, late of Heytesbury, in the county of Wilts, yeoman, William Inges, late of Heytesbury, in the county aforesaid, yeoman, [were indicted for that] on the 26th July, in the 10th year of the now Lord the King (1518), with force and arms made an assault upon John Cotell, at Farley, in the county of Somerset, by the procurement and abetting of Agnes Hungerford, late of Heytesbury, in the county of Wilts, widow, at that time the wife of the aforesaid John Cotell. And a certain linen scarf called a kerchier (*quandam flameam lineam vocatam 'a kerchier'*) which the aforesaid William and William then and there held in their hands, put round the neck of the aforesaid John Cotell, and with the aforesaid linen scarf him, the said John Cotell, then and there feloniously did throttle, suffocate, and strangle, so that the aforesaid John Cotell immediately died, and so the aforesaid William Maghewe [Mathewe] and William Inges, by the procurement and abetting of the aforesaid Agnes, did then and there feloniously murder, &c., the aforesaid John Cotell, against the peace of the Lord the King, and afterwards the aforesaid William, and William, the body of the aforesaid John Cotell did then and there put into a certain fire in the furnace of the kitchen in the Castle of Farley aforesaid, and the body of the same John in the fire aforesaid in the Castle of Farley aforesaid, in the county of Somerset aforesaid, did burn and consume.' The indictment charged that Agnes Hungerford, otherwise called Agnes Cotell, late of Heytesbury, in the county of Wilts, widow, late the wife of the aforesaid John Cotell, well knowing that the aforesaid William Mathewe and William Inges had done the felony and murder aforesaid, did receive, comfort and aid them on 28 December 1518. Such was the indictment, 'which said indictment the now Lord the King afterwards for certain reasons caused to come before him to be determined, &c.' All three accused were committed to the Tower of London: 'and now, to wit, on Thursday next after the quinzaine of St Martin [27 November 1522], in the same term, before the Lord the King at Westminster, in their proper persons came the aforesaid William Mathewe, William Inges, and Agnes Hungerford, brought here to the bar by Sir Thomas Lovell, Knight, Constable of the Tower of London, by virtue of the writ of the Lord the King to him thereupon directed.' So they were brought to trial, and all found guilty. William Mathewe and Lady Agnes Hungerford were sentenced to be hanged; William Inges pleaded benefit of clergy. The plea was contested on the ground that he had committed bigamy, by which he lost his right to claim his clergy. The question was referred to the Bishop of Salisbury, who proved that Inges was a bigamist, and Inges was therefore also sentenced to be hanged. There is no record of a third execution; the servant hanged at the same time as Lady Agnes Hungerford was therefore William Mathewe. The story is still incomplete.

In 2012 the castle site remains, a haunting, well-preserved ruin run by English Heritage. It is a Scheduled Monument and a Grade I listed building.

1525 In the last moneth called December were taken certain traytors in the citie of Coventry, one called Fraunces Philippe schoolemaster ... and one Christopher Pykeryng clerke of ye Larder, and one Antony Maynuile gentleman, which by the persuasion of the sayd Fraunces Philip, entended to have taken the kynges treasure of his subsidie as the Collectors of the same came towarde London, and then to have araised men and taken the castle of Kylingworth, and then to have made battaile against the kyng: wherfore the sayd Fraunces, Christopher and Anthony wer hanged, drawen and quartered at Tyborne the 6 day of Februarye, the residue that were taken, were sent to the citie of Coventry and there wer executed. One of the kynges Henchmen called Dygby which was one of the conspirators fled the realme, and after had his pardon. (Hall, p. 673).

1535 Proceedings were taken against the London Carthusians for refusing to admit Henry's claim to be supreme head of the Church. In the London House were at this time Father Robert Lawrence, Prior of Beauvale, and Father Augustine Webster, Prior of Axholme; Beauvale and Axholme being two other Carthusian monasteries. Together with Father Houghton, Prior of the London House, Father Lawrence and Father Webster were brought to trial and condemned. Let Chauncy [Sir Henry Chauncy, a historian, 1632–1719] tell the story of their execution; with little variation it may stand for that of all the Catholic martyrs from 1535 to 1681:

Being brought out of prison [the Tower] they were thrown down on a hurdle and fastened to it, lying at length on their backs, and so lying on the hurdle, they were dragged at the heels of horses through the city until they came to Tyburn, a place where, according to custom, criminals are executed, which is distant from the prison one league, or a French mile. Who can relate what grievous things, what tortures they endured on that whole journey, where one while the road lay over rough and hard, at another through wet and muddy places, which exceedingly abounded. On arrival at the place of execution our holy Father was the first loosed, and then the executioner, as the custom is, bent his knee before him, asking pardon for the cruel work he had to do ... beholding the benignity of so holy a man, how gently and moderately he spoke to the executioner, how sweetly he embraced and kissed him, and how piously he prayed for him and for all the bystanders. Then on being ordered to mount the ladder to the gibbet, where he was to be hanged, he meekly obeyed. Then one of the King's Council, who stood there with many thousand people, who came together to witness the sight, asked him if he would submit to the king's command and the Act of Parliament, for if he would he should be pardoned. The holy Martyr of Christ answered: 'I call Almighty God, and I beseech you all in the terrible Day of Judgment, to bear witness, that being here about to die, I publicly declare that not through any pertinacity, malice, or rebellious spirit, do I commit this disobedience and denial of the will of our lord the king, but solely through fear of God, lest I should offend His Supreme Majesty; because our holy mother, the Church, has decreed and determined otherwise than as your king and his Parliament have ordained; wherefore I am bound in conscience and am prepared, and am not confounded, to endure these and all other torments that can be inflicted, rather than go against the doctrine of the Church. Pray for me, and have pity on my brethren, of whom I am the unworthy Prior.' And having said these things, he begged the executioner to wait until he had finished his prayer. Then on a sign given, the ladder was turned, and so he was hanged. Then one of the bystanders, before his holy soul left his body, cut the rope, and so falling to the ground, he began for a little space to throb and breathe. Then he was drawn to another adjoining place, where all his garments were violently torn off, and he was again extended naked on the hurdle, on whom immediately the bloody executioner laid his wicked hands. He cut open his belly, dragged out his bowels, his heart, and all else, and threw them into a fire, during which our most blessed Father not only did not cry out on account of the intolerable pain, but on the contrary, during all this time until his heart was torn out, prayed continually, and bore himself with more than human endurance, most patiently, meekly, and tranquilly, to the wonder not only of the presiding officer, but of all the people who witnessed it. Being at his last gasp, and nearly disembowelled, he cried out with a most sweet voice, 'Most sweet Jesu, have pity on me in this hour!' And, as trustworthy men have reported, he said to the tormentor, while in the act of tearing out his heart, 'Good Jesu, what will you do with my heart?' and saying this he breathed his last. Lastly, his head was cut off, and the beheaded body was divided into four parts ... our holy Father having been thus put to death the two other before-named venerable Fathers, Robert and Augustine, with another religious named Reynolds, of the Order of St Bridget, being subjected to the same most cruel death, were deprived of life, one after another; all of whose remains were thrown into cauldrons and parboiled, and afterwards put up at different places in the city.

1535 The eighteenth of June, three Monks of the Charterhouse at London, named Thomas Exmew, Humfrey Middlemore, and Sebastian Nidigate [Newdigate] were drawn to Tiborne, and there hanged and quartered for denying the Kinges supremacie.[18]

1535–7 In 1535 was introduced the first Bill for the dissolution of the monasteries: only the smaller were now touched. The Bill was passed on Henry's threat that he would have the Bill pass, or take off some of the Commons' heads. Henry had tired of Anne Boleyn, Cranmer, always equal to the occasion, 'having previously invoked the name of Christ, and having God alone before his eyes', had declared that the marriage was void and had always been so.

In 1536 broke out the first of the revolts caused by the dissolution. Henry had not yet discovered the secret of detaching from the cause of the people their natural leaders by sharing the plunder with them. The nobility and gentry had their grievances, and made common cause with the people. Henry was furious. He gave orders to 'run upon the insurgents with your forces, and with all extremity destroy, burn, and kill man, woman and child, to the terrible example of all others'. The chief monks were to be hanged on long pieces of timber out of the steeples. Later, when the revolt had spread to Yorkshire, he wrote: 'you must cause such dreadful execution upon a good number of the inhabitants, hanging them on trees, quartering them, and setting their heads and quarters in every town, as shall be a fearful warning'. In summing up these operations, Cromwell, with a pleasant wit, speaks of the execution of the rest at 'Thyf bourne'. The story of the rest will follow. It may well be doubted whether in the history of civilised communities there is any record of a social cataclysm, not resulting from war or pestilence, so terrible as that which overwhelmed the commons of England after the dissolution of the monasteries, followed by measures of plunder extending through the reign of Edward VI. Marks tells us that a calculation based upon the statements of this same writer on the 'Decay of England' gives 675,000 persons thrown upon the country by the decay of husbandry. But to this number we must add those turned out of the monasteries, the poor, formerly maintained by the monasteries and by the yeomanry, the sick and infirm, ejected from the hospitals established for 'Christ's poor' as they are called in the act of foundation of a hospital in the thirteenth century. And this immense number out of a population estimated at 5,000,000! 'And nowe they have nothynge, but goeth about in England from dore to dore, and axe theyr almose for Goddes sake. And because they will not begge, some of them doeth steale, and then they be hanged.' Great numbers flocked to London, seeking in vain redress of their grievances. This was the great time of Tyburn. 'I was desirous to heare of execution done for there was three wekes sessions at newgate, and fourth nyghte Sessions at the Marshialshy, and so forth.' That is, sessions every three weeks at the one place and every two weeks at the other. Never had the gallows been so crowded. In the sentence quoted on the title-page of this book,

Sir Thomas More, writing in Latin in 1516, had said that twenty were 'sometimes' hanged together upon one gallows. In the English translation, first published in 1551: 'So had the gallows thriven!' A contemporary report states that 'in one way or another Henry did in the course of his reign destroy seventy-two thousand persons'. It is said that 'over 5,000 men were hanged within the space of six years' in a district of North Wales. As if to prove the point we find the following.

1537 The nine and twentith of March were 12 men of Lincolne drawne to Tyborne, and there hanged and quartered, five were priests, and 7 were lay men, i. one was an Abbot, a suffragan, doctor Mackerel; another was the vicar of Louth in Lincolnshire, & two priests. Alsoe, the 17 daye of Maye, were arraynad at Westmynster these persons followinge: Doctor Cokerell, prieste and chanon, John Pykeringe, layman, the Abbot of Gervase [Jervaulx] and an Abbott condam [quondam] of Fountens, of the order of pyed monkes, the Prior of Bridlington, Chanon, Docter John Pykeringe, fryer of the order of prechers, and Nicholas Tempeste, esquire, all which persons were that daye condemned of highe treason, and had judgment for the same. And, the 25 daye of Maye, beinge the Frydaye in Whytsonweke, Sir John Bolner, Sir Stephen Hamerton, knightes, were hanged and heddyd, Nicholas Tempeste, esquier, Docter Cokerell, preiste, Abbott condam of Fountens, and Docter Pykeringe, fryer, ware drawen from the Towre of London to Tyburne, and ther hanged, boweld, and quartered, and their heddes sett on London Bridge and diverse gates in London. And the same daye Margaret Cheyney, other wife to Bolmer called ['which' says Hall, 'some reported was not his wife but his paramour'] was drawen after them from the Tower of London into Smythfyld, and there brente, (*burnt*) according to hir judgment, God pardon her sowle, being the Frydaye in Whytson weeke; she was a very fayre creature and bewtyfull … The second daie of June, being Saterdaie after Trinitie Sundaie, this yeare Sir Thomas Percey, knight, and brother to the Earle of Northumberland, was drawen from the Tower of London to Tiburne, and their hanged and beheaded, and Sir Francis Bigott, knight, Georg Lomeley, esquire, sonne to the Lord Lomeley, the Abbott of Gervase, and the Prior of Bridlington, were drawen from the said place to Tiburne, and their hanged and quartered,

according to their judgmente, and their heades sett on London
Bridge and other gates of London. (Stow, p. 573)

1538 In July was Edmond Coningsbey attainted of treason, for
counterfeatyng of the kynges Signe Manuell: And in August was
Edward Clifford for the same cause attainted, and both put to
execucion as traitors at Tiborne. And the Sonday after Bartelmew
day, was one Cratwell hangman of London, and two persones more
hanged at the wrestlyng place on the backesyde of Clerkenwel
besyde London, for robbyng of a bouthe in Bartholomew fayre, at
which execution was above twentie thousand people as I my self
iudged (*Hall's Chronicles*, p. 826).

1538–9 The third daie of Novembre were Henry Marques of
Excester (Exeter) & earle of Devonshire and sir Henry Pole knight
and lorde Mountagew and Sir Edward Nevell brother to the Lorde
Burgany sent to the tower which thre wer accused by sir Gefferei
Pole brother to the lord Mountagew, of high treason, and the two
lordes were arreigned the last day of Decembre, at Westminster
before the lord Awdeley of Walden, lord Chauncelor, and then the
high stuard of England, and there found giltie, likewise on the third
day after was arreigned Sir Edward Nevel, Sir Gefferey Pole and two
priestes called Croftes and Collins, and one holand a Mariner and all
attainted, and the ninth day of Januarie [1539] were the saied two
lordes and Sir Edward Nevell behedded at the tower hill, and the two
priestes and Holande were drawen to Tiborne, and there hanged and
quartered, and sir Gefferey Pole was pardoned (Hall, p. 827).

1539 The eight and twentie daie of Aprill, began a Parliament at
Westminster, in the which Margaret countesse of Salsbury, Gertrude
wife to the Marques of Excester, Reignold Poole, a Cardinall brother
to the lorde Mountagew, Sir Adrian Foskew [Fortescue] & Thomas
Dingley Knight of saynt Johnes, & diverse other wer attainted of
high treason, which Foskew and Dynglei wer the tenth daie of Juli
behedded. According to the Grey Friars Chronicle and Wriothesley's
Chronicle they were beheaded at Tower Hill on the 9th July, and
that same day was drawne to Tyborne ii. of their servanttes, and ther
hongyd and quarterd for tresoun.

1540 Also this same yere was the 16 day of Marche was one
Somer and 3 vagabondes with hym drawne, hangyd and qwarterd
for clippynge of golde at Tyborne.[19]

1540 Dr Johnson blamed the Government of his day for suppressing the processions to Tyburn: 'the public was gratified by a procession'. From this point of view Henry VIII was an ideal monarch, though it is open to doubt whether the burnings at Smithfield and the disembowellings at Tyburn were not so frequent as to satiate the lovers of these spectacles. Thus on 30 July 1540, two Doctors of Divinity and a parson were burnt in Smithfield, and on the same day another Doctor and two priests were hanged on a gallows at Saint Bartholomew's Gate, beheaded and quartered. Five days later the spectacle was offered of other seven or perhaps eight despatched at Tyburn.

1540, August 4 The 4 of August, Thomas Empson sometime a monke of Westminster, which had bin prisoner in Newgate more than three yeeres, was brought before the Justices of gaole deliverie at Newgate, and for that hee would not aske the King pardon for denying his supremacie, nor be sworne therto, his monkes coole was plucked from his backe, and his body repried till the King were informed of his obstinacie. Nothing more is told us of Empson, but it has been supposed that he was executed in this batch.[20] 'The same 4 of August were drawn to Tyborne 6 persons and one lead betwixt twaine, to wit, Laurence Cooke, prior of Doncaster, William Home a lay brother of the Charterhouse of London, Giles Home gentleman, Clement Philip gentleman of Caleis, & servant to the L. Lisle, Edmond Bromholme priest, chaplaine to the said L. Lisley, Darby Gening, Robert Bird, all hanged and quartered, and had beene attainted by parliament, for deniall of the Kings supremacie.[21]

1540 On the 22 daie of December, was Raufe Egerton servant to the Lorde Audeley lorde Chaunccellor, hanged, drawen, and quartered, for counterfetyng of the kynges greate Seale, in a signet, whiche was never seen, and sealed a great number of Licenses for Denizens, and one Thomas Harman that wrote theim, was executed: for the statute made the last parliament sore bounde the straungiers, whiche wer not Denizens, whiche caused theim to offre to Egerton, greate sommes of money, the desire whereof caused hym to practise that whiche brought hym to the ende, that before is declared.[22]

1541, June 28 There was executed at saint Thomas Waterings three gentlemen, John Mantell, John Frowds, and George Roidon: they died for a murther committed in Sussex (as their indictement imported) in companie of Thomas Fines Lord Dacres of the south. The truth whereof was thus. The said Lord Dacres, through the lewd persuasion of some of them, as hath beene reported, meaning to hunt in the parke of Nicholas Pelham esquire at Laughton, in the same countie of Sussex, being accompanied with the said Mantell, Frowds, and Roidon, John Cheinie and Thomas Isleie gentlemen, Richard Middleton and John Goldwell yeomen, passed from his house of Hurstmonseux, the last of Aprill in the night season, toward the same parke, where they intended so to hunt: and comming unto a place called Pikehaie in the parish of Hillingleie, they found one John Busbrig, James Busbrig, and Richard Sumner standing togither; and as it fell out through quarelling, there insued a fraie betwixt the said lord Dacres and his companie on the one partie, and the said John and James Busbrig and Richard Sumner on the other: insomuch that the said John Busbrig received such hurt, that he died thereof the second of Maie next insuing. Whereupon, as well the said lord Dacres as those that were there with him, and diverse other likewise that were appointed to go another waie to meet them at the said parke, were indicted of murther; and the seaven and twentith of June the lord Dacres himselfe was arreigned before the lord Audleie of Walden then lord chancellor, sitting that daie as high steward of England, with other peeres of the realme about him, who then and there condemned the said lord Dacres to die for that transgression. And afterward the nine and twentith of June being saint Peters daie, at eleven of the clocke in the forenoone, the shiriffs of London, accordinglie as they were appointed, were readie at the tower to have received the said prisoner, and him to have lead to execution on the tower hill. But as the prisoner should come forth of the tower, one Heire a gentleman of the lord chancellor's house came, and in the kings name commanded to staie the execution till two of the clocke in the afternoone, which caused manie to thinke that the king would have granted his pardon. But neverthelesse, at three or the clocke in the same afternoone, he was brought forth of the tower, and deliveredto the shiriffs, who lead him on foot betwixt them unto Tiburne, where he died. His bodie was buried in the church of saint Sepulchers. He was not past foure and twentie yeeres of age, when he came through this great mishap to his end, for whome manie sore lamented, and likewise for the other three gentlemen, Mantell,

Frowds, and Roidon. But for the said yoong lord, being a right towardlie gentleman, and such a one, as manie had conceived great hope of better proofe, no small mone and lamentation was made; the more indeed, for that it was thought he was induced to attempt such follie, which occasioned his death, by some light heads that were then about him.

1542 The 20 of March was one Clement Dyer, a vintner, drawen to Tyburne for treason, and hanged and quartered.[23] Early historian, Hall says that 'greate moane was made for them al, but moste specially for Mantel, who was as wittie, and as towarde a gentleman, as any was in the realme, and a manne able to have dooen good service.

1542, December 10 At this tyme the Quene late before maried to the kyng called Quene Katheryne, was accused to the Kyng of dissolute Huring, (*whoring*) before her mariage, with Fraunces Diram (*Dereham*) and that was not secretely, but many knewe it. And sithe her Mariage, she was vehemently suspected with Thomas Culpeper, whiche was brought to her Chamber at Lyncolne, in August laste, in the Progresse tyme, by the Lady of Rocheforde, and were there together alone, from a leven of the Clocke at Nighte, till foure of the Clocke in the Mornyng, and to hym she gave a Chayne, and a riche Cap. Upon this the kyng removed to London and she was sent to Sion (*Abbey*) and there kept close, but yet served as Quene. And for the offence confessed by Culpeper and Diram, thei were put to death at Tiborne.[24] Culpeper was headed, his body buried at Saint Sepulchers Church by Newgate: Derham was quartered &c.[25]

1544 The 7 of March, Garmaine Gardner, and Larke parson of Chelsey, were executed at Tyborne, for denying the kings supremacie, with them was executed, for other offences, one Singleton. And shortly after, Ashbey was likewise executed for the supremacie.[26]

Henry VIII was succeeded by his only legitimate son, the boy, King Edward VI in 1547. Two years later the peasants rose against their oppressors. Here are echoes of the risings in the West and in Norfolk.

1549 Item the 27 day of the same monythe [August] was 3 persons drawyn, hangyd, and qwarterd at Tyborne that came owte of the West contrey.[27]

1550 The 27 of January, Humfrey Arundell esquire, Thomas Holmes, Winslowe and Bery Captaines of the rebels in Devonshire, were hanged and quartered at Tyborne.[28]

1550 The 10 of February one Bel a Suffolke man, was hanged and quartered at Tyborne, for mooving a new rebellion in Suffolke & Essex.[29]

The following is from Henry Machyn's Diary, 1550 to 1563 (Camden Society, 1848). Machyn's spelling is barely decipherable; it has been amended to keep the sense, and allow some understanding.

1552 The 2 day of May ... the sam day was hangyd at Tyborne 9 fello[ns]

The 11day of July [was] hangyd one James Ellys, the grett pykkepurs that ever was, and cutt-purs, and 7 more for theyfft, at Tyburne.

1553 The 21 day of the same monyth [January] rode unto [Tyburn] 2 felons, serten was for kyllyng of a gentylman [of] sir Edward North knyght, in Charturhowsse Cheyr [Churchyard?] the 7 yere of kyng Edward the 6' (Machyn, p. 30). 'Rod' means rode in a cart. Edward died on July 6, 1553. The rebellion in favour of Lady Jane Grey was quickly put down, and Mary made her entry into London on August 3. At the end of January 1554, broke out Sir Thomas Wyatt's rebellion. It was suppressed, but not till after Wyatt had made his way into the heart of the City. The gallows of Tyburn was supplemented by numerous others: 'The 18 day of May was drawne a-pon a sled a proper man named Wylliam Thomas from the Towre unto Tyborne ... he was clarke to the consell; and he was hangyd, and after his hed stryken of, and then quartered; and the morow after his hed was sett on London bryge, and 3 quarters set over Cripullgate (Machyn, p. 63).

1555 The tenth of May, William Constable, alias Fetherstone, a Millers sonne about the age of eighteene yeares, who had published King Edw. the 6 to be alive, and sometime named himselfe to bee K. Edw. the 6. was taken at Eltham in Kent, and conveyed to Hampton court, where being examined by the counsell, hee required pardon, & said he wist not what hee did, but as he was perswaded by many; from thence he was sent to the Marshalsea, & the 22 of May he was caried in a cart through London to Westminster with a paper on his head, wherein was written, that he had named himselfe to be king Edw. After he had beene carried about Westminster hall before the Judges, he was whipped a bout the pallace, and through Westminster into Smithfield, and then banished into the North, in which countrie hee was borne, and had beene sometime Lackey to sir Peter Mewtas (Stow, p. 626). But William's whipping did not cure him of his folly: The 26 of February [1556] Willi. Constable alias Fetherstone was arraigned in the Guild hall of London, who had caused letters to bee cast abrode, that king Edward was alive, and to some he shewed himselfe to be king Edward, so that many persons both menne and women were troubled by him, for the which sedition the said William had bin once whipped and delivered, as is aforesaid: But now he was condemned, and the 13 of March he was drawne, hanged and quartered at Tyborne (Stow, p. 628).

Mary died in 1558, and Elizabeth I came to the throne.

1570 The 27 of May, Thomas Norton and Christopher [Norton], of Yorkshire, being both condemned of high treason, for the late rebellion in the North, were drawne from the Tower of London to Tiborne and there hanged, headed, and quartered (Stow, p. 666).

A tract, the 'Confessions' of Thomas Norton and Christopher Norton, reprinted in *State Trials vol. i., 1083–6*, contains particulars of these executions. Thomas, the uncle of Christopher, was first hanged and quartered, in the presence of his nephew. Then the hangman executed his office on Christopher, and being hanged a little while, and then cut down, the butcher opened him, and as he took out his bowels, he cried and said, 'Oh, Lord, Lord, have mercy upon me!' and so yielded up the ghost. Then being likewise quartered, as the other was, and their bowels burned, as the manner is, their quarters were put into a basket provided for the purpose, and so carried to Newgate, where they were parboiled; and afterwards their heads set on London Bridge, and their quarters set upon sundry gates of the city of London.

1570 The 25 May in the morning, was found hanging at the bishop of Londons palace gate in Paules church-yard, a Bull (*papal proclamation*) which lately had beene sent from Rome containing diverse horrible treasons against the Queenes majesty for the which one John Felton was shortly after apprehended, and committed to the tower of London ... The fourth of August ... was arraigned at Guild hal of London John Felton, for hanging a bull at the gate of the bishop of Londons palace, and also two young men, for coyning and clipping of coine, who all were found guilty of high treason, and had iudgment to be drawne, hanged and quartered. The eight of August, John Felton was drawne from Newgate into Paules Churchyeard, and there hanged on a gallowes new set up that morning before the Bishoppes palace gate, and being cut downe alive, he was bowelled and quartered. After this time the same morning the sherifs returned to Newgate, and so to Tiborne with two young men which were executed for coyning and clipping as is aforesaid.[30]

1571 The execution of Dr John Story is one of the horrors of Tyburn: Dr Story was a bitter persecutor under Mary. After the accession of Elizabeth, Story had more than one narrow escape. In 1563 he was imprisoned in the Marshalsea, whence he escaped, and, with the aid of the chaplain of the Spanish Ambassador, fled to Flanders. The Spanish Ambassador disclaimed knowledge of the matter, but it may well be that the English Government was nettled, and readily lent itself to a plan for capturing Story. In his adopted country he received a place in the customs. On a certain day in August, 1570, he was invited to examine a ship at Bergen-op-Zoom. While he was busy in the hold the hatches were shut down on him, the sail was hoisted, and the ship sailed for Yarmouth with Story on board. The capture was a great event. 'The locks and bolts of the Lollards' Tower were broken off at the death of queen Mary, and never since repaired. Now they were repaired for the reception of Dr Story'. He was executed at Tyburn on June 1 1571. He was the object of general execration: care was probably taken that he should suffer all the torments of the horrible sentence. He was let down from the gallows alive, and while the executioner was 'rifling among his bowels' Story rose and dealt him a blow.

1581 The 18 of July, Everard Haunce [Hanse] a seminary priest, was in the Sessions hall in the olde Baily arraigned, where he affirmed that himselfe was subiect to the Pope in ecclesiasticall causes, and that the Pope hath now the same authoritie here in England that hee had an hundred yeeres past, with other trayterous speeches, for the which hee was condemned to bee drawne, hanged, bowelled, and quartered, and was executed accordingly on the last of July.[31]

1581 On the 20 of November, Edm. Champion [Campion] Jesuit, Ralfe Sherwine, Lucas Kerbie, Edward Rishton, Thomas Coteham, Henrie Orton, Robert Johnson, and James Bosgraue, were brought to the high bar at Westminster, where they were severally, and all together indicted upon high treason, for that contrary both to love and dutie, they forsooke their native countrey, to liue beyond the seas under the Popes obedience, as at Rome, Rheimes, and diverse other places, where (the pope having with other princes practised the death and deprivation of our most gracious princesse and utter subversion of her state and kingdome, to advance his most abominable religion) these menne having vowed their alleagiance to the pope, to obey him in all causes whatsoever, being there, gave their consent, to ayd him in this most trayterous determination. And for this intent and purpose they were sent over to seduce the harts of her majesties loving subiects, and to conspire and practise her graces death, as much as in them lay, against a great daie, set & appoynted, when the generall havocke should be made, those onely reserved thatjioyned with them. This laid to their charge, they boldly denied, but by a jurie they were approoved guiltie, and had judgement to bee hanged, bowelled, and quartered.[32]

The account of the executions of some of these will follow. According to Camden, Elizabeth did not at all believe them guilty of plotting the destruction of the country; they were tried and executed to take away the fear which had possessed many men's minds that religion would be altered if she married a foreign prince.

1581 The first of December, Edmond Champion [Campion] Jesuit, Ralfe Sherwine, and Alexander Brian seminary priests, were drawne from the tower of London to Tyborne, & there hanged, bowelled and quartered.[33]

1582 On the 28 day of May, Thomas Ford, John Shert, & Robert Johnson, priests, having bin before indicted, arraigned, and condemned for high treason intended, as yee have heard of Champion and other, were drawne from the Tower to Tiborne, and there hanged, bowelled, and quartered. And on the 30 Luke Kirby, William Filby, Thomas Cottam, and Laurence Richardson, were for the like treason in the same place likewise executed.[34]

1584 February 12. The 7 of February, were arraygned at Westminster John Fen [James Fenn] George Haddocke [Haydock],

John Munden, John Nutter, and Thomas Hemerford, all five found guiltie of high treason, in being made priestes beyond the seas, and by the Popes authoritie, since a statute made in Anno primo of her majesties raygne, and hadde Judgement to be hanged, bowelled, & quartered: which were all executed at Tyborne on the 12.of February.[35]

1584 The 21of May, Francis Throckmorton Esquire was arraygned in the Guild hall of the cittie of London, where being found guiltie of high Treason, hee was condemned, & had judgement to be drawne, hanged, bowelled, & quartered. The 10 of July next following, the same Francis Throckmorton was conveyed by water from the Tower of London, to the Blacke fryers stayres, and from thence by land to the sessions hall in the Olde baily without Newgate, where hee was delivered to the sheriffes of London, laid on a hurdle, drawne to Tyborne, & there executed according to his judgement.[36]

1588, August 26 At the sessions hall without Newgate of London, were condemned 6 persons, for being made priests beyond the seas, & remaining in this realme contrary to a statute thereof made, 4. temporall men for being reconciled to the Romane Church; & 4 other for releeving & abetting the others. And on the 28. W. Deane, & H. Webley, were hanged at ye Miles end. W. Gunter at the Theater, R. Moorton & Hugh Moore at Lincolnes Inne fields, Tho.Acton [Thomas Holford] at Clarkenwell, Tho. Felton & James Clarkson [Claxton] betweene Brainford (*Brentford*) & Hounslow. And on the 30.of August, R. Flower, Ed. Shelley, R. Leigh, R. Martine, I. Roch, & Margaret Ward gentlewoman (which Margaret hadde conveyed a cord to a priest in Bridewell, whereby he let himself downe & escaped) were hanged at Tiborne.[37]

1591 The 10 of December 3 Seminary priests for being in this realm contrary to the statute and 4 others, for relieving them, were executed, two of them, to wit, a Seminary named Ironmonger [Edmund Genings], and Swithen Wels, gentleman, in Grayes Inne field, Blaston [Polydore Plasden] and White, Seminaries, and three other their abbettors at Tyborne (Stow, p. 764). [The names of these three others were, Bryan Lacy, Sydney Hodson, and John Mason].

In *The Life and Death of Mr Edmund Geninges Priest, Crowned with Martyrdome at London the 10 day of November (sic) in the yeare MDXCI* (S. Omers, 1614), is an account of the trial and execution. Wells on returning to London found his house shut up, and was told that his wife was in Newgate. He went to Justice Yonge to ask for restitution of wife and keys, when he was at once sent to Newgate. He pleaded that he was not aware of the doings in his house. 'Then the Justice … told him in playne termes, he came time inough to taste of the sauce, although he were ignorant how the meate savoured.' The manner of the execution of Edmund Genings is thus told: 'he being ripped up, & his bowelles cast into the fire, if credit may be given to hundreds of People standing by, and to the Hangman himselfe, the blessed Martyr uttered (his hart being in the Executioners hand) these words, Sancte Gregori ora pro me, which the Hangman hearing, with open mouth swore this damnable oath; Gods woundes, See his hart is in my hand, and yet Gregory in his mouth; egregious Papist!'

1593 The 21 of March, Henry Barrow, gentleman, John Greenewood clarke, Daniel Studley girdler, Saxio Billot, gentleman, Robert Bowley, Fishmonger, were indicted of Felony at the sessions hall without Newgate beefore the Major, the two lord Chiefe Justices of both benches, and sundry of the Judges & other commissioners of Oyer and determiner; the sayd Barrow and Greenwood for writing sundry seditious bookes, tending to the slaunder of the Queene and state; Studley, Billot, and Bowley, for publishing and setting foorth the same Bookes, and on the 23 they were all arraygned at Newgate, found guiltie, and had judgement. On the last of March Henry Barrow and John Greenwood were brought to Tyborne in a carre, and there fastened to the Gallowes, but being stayde and returned for the time, they were there hanged on the sixt of Aprill.[38]

1594 The last of February, Rodericke Loppez, a Portingale (*Portuguese*) … professing physicke, was arraygned in the Guild hall of London, found guiltie, and had iudgement as of high treason, for conspiring her Majesties destruction by poison. The 7 of June, Rodericke Loppez, with the other two Portingales … were convayd by water from Westminster to the Bishoppe of Winchesters staires in Southwarke, from thence to the King's bench, there laid on hurdles, and convayd by the Sheriffes of London over the bridge, up to Leaden hall, and so to Tyborne, & there hanged, cut downe alive, holden downe by strength of men, dismembred, bowelled, headed & quartered, their quarters set on the gates of the cittie (Stow).

Camden's account of this affair (greatly abbreviated) is that certain Spaniards prevailed on Roderigo Lopez, a Portuguese Jew, the Queen's physician, Stephen Ferreira Gama, and Emanuel Loisie, both Portuguese, to poison the Queen. The convictions were obtained on the strength of confessions. 'How far,' says Lingard, 'These confessions made in the Tower, and probably on the rack, are deserving of credit, may be doubted' (ed. 1849, vol. vi. p. 554). It is a strange feature in the case that while Camden, like Stow, speaks of the execution of all three, Lingard shows that Ferreira was saved. The probability seems to be that Lopez fell a victim to the rivalry between Essex and the Cecils, each eager to prove greater zeal in the Queen's service. Arising out of similar plots, real or pretended, were at this time other executions.

1598 The 25 of January, one named Ainger was hanged at Tyborne, for wilfully and secretly murthering of his owne father a Gentleman and Counsellor of the Law at Graies Inne, in his chamber there' (Stow, p. 786). About the middle of November, 1597, a body was found floating on the Thames, and was identified as that of Richard Ainger, 'a double reader' of Gray's Inn, who had been missing for some time. On view of the body the surgeons gave it as their opinion that Ainger had met his death, not by drowning but by suffocation, and that the body had been thrown into the river after death. Suspicion attached to one of his sons, Richard, and to Edward Ingram, a porter of the Inn. The Privy Council addressed a letter to Mr Recorder of London, Mr Topcliffe, Nicholas Fuller, William Gerrard, and Mr Altham, requiring them to examine strictly the two suspected persons, 'and yf by those persuasions and other meanes you shall use you shall not be able to bring them to confesse the truthe of this horrible facte, then we require you to put them both or either of them to the manacles in Bridewell, that by compulsory meanes the truthe of this wicked murther may be discovered, and who were complices and privy to this confederacy and fact.'[39]

1598 On the tenth of July, 19 persons for fellony were hanged at Tyborne, & one pressed to death at Newgate of London.[39]

1601 After the capture of the earl of Essex on 12 February, Thomas Lea (a kinsman of Sir Henry Lea's, who had wore the Honour of the Garter) told Sir Robert Crofts, Captain of a Man of War, that 'twould be a glorious Enterprize for six brave mettl'd

Fellows to go to the Queen, and compel her to discharge Essex, [*and the*] earl of Southampton, and the rest that were in Prison. He was a Man himself of great Assurance and Resolution, had Commanded a Company in Ireland, was very intimate with Tir Oen, and an absolute Creature of the Earl of Essex's. This did Crofts immediately discover to the Council insomuch that Lea was sought for, and found in the dusk of the Evening about the door of the Queen's Privy-Chamber. He seem'd very Thoughtful, was extreamly Pale, and in a great Sweat, and frequently ask'd, Whether her Majesty was ready to go to Supper? And, Whether the Council would be there? In this Posture he was seiz'd and Examin'd, the next day had his Trial, and by Crofts's Evidence and his own Confession, condemn'd and carried away to Tyburn, where he own'd that he had been indeed a great Offender; but as to this Design, was very Innocent; and having moreover protested, that he had never entertain'd the least ill Thought against the Queen, he was there executed. And this, as the Times were, appear'd a very seasonable piece of Rigour'.

1601 The 22 of February, Marke Bakworth [Barkworth], and Thomas Filcoks [Roger Filcock], were drawne to Tyborne, and there hanged, & quartered, for comming into the Realme contrary to the statute. Also the same day, and in the same place, was hanged a Gentlewoman, called Mistris Anne Line, a widow, for relieving a priest contrary to the same statute (Stow, p. 794).

The crime for which Mistress Line suffered was that, Mass having been said in her house, she assisted the priest in his escape. 'Mr Barkwey cominge to the hurdle prayed and with a chearfull voyce and smylinge countenance sunge all the waye he went to execution. The 26th daye of Februarie 1600 [1601], beinge the first Friday in Lent, the said Mr Barkwey was brought to Tyborne there to be executed. Cominge up into the carte in his blacke habite, his hoode being taken of, his heade beinge all shaven but for a rounde circle on the nether parte of his heade, and his other garment taken of also, beinge turned into his sherte, having a pare of hose of haere, most joyfully and smylingly looked up directly to the heavens and blessed him with the signe of the crosse, sayinge, "In nomine Patris, Filii et Spiritus Sancti, Amen." Then he turned himselfe towardes the gallowe tree wheron he was to suffer, made the signe of the crosse theron and kissed it and the rope also, the which beinge put about his necke, he turned himselfe and with a chearfull smylinge countenance and pleasant voyce sunge in manner and forme followinge, "I doe confesse that I am one of the Blessed Societie after the holy order of St Benedicte." The minister called on him to be penitent for his sinnes, and he said, "Hold thy peace, thou arte a simple fellowe." Then the minister willed him to remember that Christ Jesus dyed for him. And he, elevatinge his eyes to heaven and holdinge the rope in his handes being fastened together so highe as he could reache, aunswered "and so doe I for him, and I would I had a thousand, thousand lyves to bestowe upon him in this cause," sayinge "et majorem charitatem nemo habet." And then turninge himselfe againe, sunge as before, and desired all Catholiques to praye for him, and he would praye for them. And beinge asked if he would praye for the Queene he saied, "God blesse her, and send her and me to meete joyfully in heaven," and prayed also for Mr Recorder who pronounced judgment against him, and for Mr Wade, Ingleby, Parrat, and Singleton, who were the prosecutors of his death. And the carte beinge drawne awaye, in his goinge of from the carte saied the same wordes as before, "Haec est dies Domini; gaudeamus in ea" and beinge presently cut downe, he stoode uprighte on his feete and strugled with the Executioners, cryinge, "Lord, Lord, Lord," and beinge holden by the strengthe of the executioners on the hurdle in dismembringe of him he cryed, "O God," and so he was quartered. There was executed also one Mistriss Lynde [Anne Line], condemned at the Sessions house the 26th day of February for the escape of a supposed priest. Her weakness was suche that she was carried to the said Sessions betwixt two in a chaire. There was also condemned with her one Ralphe Slyvell for rescuinge the said supposed priest, but repryved. The said Mistriss Lynde, carried the next daye to her execution, many tymes in the waye was stayed and urged by the minister who urged what meanes he could to perswade her to convert from her professed faithe and opinion, most constantlie persevered therin and so was brought to the place of execution and there shewed the cause of her cominge thither, and beinge further urged amongest other thinges by the minister that she had bene a common receavor of many priestes she aunswered, "Where I have received one I would to God I had bene able to have received a thousand." She behaved herself most meekely, patiently, and vertuously to her last breath. She kissed the gallowes and before and after her private prayers blessinge herself, the carte was drawne awaye, and she then made the signe of the crosse uppon her, and after that never moved.'

1603. The 17 of Februarie, W. Anderson [or Richardson] a Seminary Priest was drawne to Tyborne and there hanged, bowelled and quartered, for being found in England contrary to the statute of Anno. 27.[40]

Anderson was the last of Elizabeth's victims; she died a few weeks later.

James I, the son of Mary Queen of Scotts, succeeded Elizabeth in 1603. In 1605 came the Gunpowder Plot; none of the conspirators suffered at Tyburn.

1608 The 2 of Aprill, George Jervis [Gervase or Jarvis] a Seminary priest, according to his judgement was executed at Tyborne (Stow). The 23 of June, Thomas Garnet, a Jesuite was executed at Tyborne, having favor offred him, if he would have taken the oath of alleageance aforesayd, but he refused it.[41]

Thomas Garnet was related to Father Henry Garnet, executed for the Gunpowder Plot in 1606. Thomas Garnet was convicted on evidence that while a prisoner in the Tower he had written in several places 'Thomas Garnet priest'. The Earl of Exeter, one of the Privy Council, present at the execution, would not suffer the rope to be cut till the victim was quite dead.[42]

1610, December 10 John Roberts, and Thomas Somers, or Watson, or Wilson. These were priests. Roberts was apprehended for the fifth time at Mass and hurried away in his vestments. Somers had been deported, together with about a score of priests, earlier in the year, but returned to England. With Roberts and Somers were executed sixteen persons condemned for various offences. The priests were suffered to hang till they were dead and then bowelled, beheaded, and quartered, and buried with the sixteen in a pit.[43]

1612 William Scot and Richard Newport, or Smith. These were missionary priests who had been banished but returned to England. The burning of Protestant heretics went on through the reigns of Elizabeth and James; 'the fires of Smithfield' were not extinguished by the death of 'Bloody Mary'. Anabaptists and Arians were burnt, the printers, the distributors, even in one case the binder of books 'seditiously penned against the Book of Common Prayer' were hanged. It is painful to find the genial Howell writing thus in 1635: 'I rather pity than hate Turk or Infidel, for they are of the same metal and bear the same stamp as I do, tho the Inscriptions differ. If I hate any, 'tis those Schismaticks that puzzle the sweet peace of our Church, so that I could be content to see an Anabaptist go to Hell on a Brownist's back.'[44]

1615 The murder of Sir Thomas Overbury is, with the possible exception of the supposed murder of Sir Edmund Berry Godfrey, a little more than sixty years later, the greatest of all English *causes célèbre*. Overbury, after leaving Oxford, made a tour on the Continent, returning from his travels a finished gentleman. In 1601, on a visit to Scotland, he met Robert Carr, then a page in a noble family. Hence arose a close intimacy destined to be fatal to Overbury. On the accession of James to the English throne, Carr, James's 'favourite', rose rapidly; he became Viscount Rochester. Carr and Overbury played into one another's hands: Carr procured a knighthood for Overbury, Overbury became the mentor of Carr, who had neither learning nor the graces of a Court. The fatal woman now comes on the scene. At the age of thirteen, Frances Howard, daughter of the Earl of Suffolk, was married to the Earl of Essex, a year older. Their friends agreed that it was yet too early for the pair to live together; the boy went on his travels, the girl to her mother. On his return, Essex found his wife acknowledged as the greatest beauty in the Court, the object of general adoration. Among her admirers was Carr, for whom she had conceived a passion which knew no bounds. Overbury had been instrumental in bringing together Carr and the lady; it was he who wrote the love-letters to which Carr owed the conquest of the countess's heart. The lady naturally hated her husband, whose return interfered with her way of life: it was only in obedience to the King's command that she consented to live with Essex. The lady and her lover formed the design of procuring a divorce from Essex, preparatory to their marriage. Overbury strongly objected; he spoke of the countess to Carr in terms which, repeated to the lady, fixed his doom. It was contrived that the King should offer to Overbury a foreign appointment. This Carr advised him to refuse, and then represented the refusal to James in such a light that on 21 April,[45] Overbury was thrown into the Tower. The lieutenant and the under-keeper of the Tower were displaced in favour of officers on whom Carr and his mistress could rely, and the work of despatching Overbury began. Poisons were procured from Franklin, a physician, by Mrs Turner, and sent in tarts and jellies to the Tower, where Weston, the under-keeper, took charge of them. Overbury was drenched with rosealgar, sublimate of mercury, arsenic, diamond powder. It was averred that he had swallowed poison enough to kill twenty men. He died on 15 September 1613. The business of the divorce now went on without hindrance. To be rid of his wife, Essex was ready enough to allow a slur to be cast on his manhood; with the aid of the lawyers, the churchmen, a complaisant jury of matrons, and a young lady who, with muffled head, impersonated the countess for the occasion, the divorce was carried through. In view of the approaching marriage, Carr was created Earl of Somerset, and on 26 December the marriage took place. With magnificent effrontery, the lady was married 'in her hair' the mark of a virgin-bride. But some time afterwards an apothecary's boy, who had been got out of the way, and was now at Flushing, began to talk of what he knew; inquiry was made, and in the end the criminals were put upon their trial.

On 23 October 1615, Richard Weston, the under-keeper of the Tower, was hanged at Tyburn. He was followed by Mrs Turner, hanged on 9 November, at the same place; on the 20th Sir Gervase Elwes, the lieutenant of the Tower, was executed on Tower Hill, and on 9 December, James Franklin, the physician, was executed at St Thomas' Waterings. In the following year the countess was tried in Westminster hall, pleaded guilty, and was condemned. The next day the earl was brought to trial by his peers in the same place, and also found guilty. Neither was executed; each received a pardon. They lived together afterwards in the same house, hating one another with a perfect hatred; the countess died of a loathsome disease. There are mysteries in the case remaining after the most careful study of the facts. In spite of all attempts made to persuade Somerset to plead guilty, and throw himself on the King's mercy, he steadfastly refused. Mr Amos inclines to believe him innocent of complicity in the murder. There are serious difficulties in the way of this theory, but it is certain that Somerset had the means of terrifying the King. Secret messages passed between the Tower and the palace, informing the king that the prisoner had threatened to refuse to go to the Court of his own will. Bacon consulted the judges as to what could be done to silence Somerset if he 'should break forth into any speech of taxing the King.' At the trial two servants were placed, one on either side of the prisoner, with a cloak on his arm. Their orders were that if Somerset 'flew out on the King', they should instantly throw the cloaks over his head, and carry him by force from the bar. Was James an accomplice in the murder of Overbury? Mayerne, the King's physician, attended Overbury in the Tower and prescribed for him. Mayerne was not produced as a witness, nor were his prescriptions put in evidence. Or is the mystery connected with the death of Prince Henry, James's son? The Prince was seized with sudden illness almost immediately after dining with his father. 'In Mayerne's collection of cases for which he wrote prescriptions,' says Mr Amos, 'everything that relates to Prince Henry's last illness is torn out of the book.' We can but fall back on the certainty that Somerset had it in his power to make some revelation of which James was terribly afraid.

1618, March 1 Touching the News of the Time: Sir George Villiers, the new Favourite, tapers up apace, and grows strong at Court: His Predecessor the Earl of Somerset hath got a Lease of 90 years for his Life, and so hath his Articulate Lady, called so, for articling against the frigidity and impotence of her former Lord. She was afraid that Coke, the Lord Chief Justice (who had used such extraordinary art and industry in discovering all the circumstances of the poisoning of Overbury) would have made white Broth of them, but that the Prerogative kept them from the Pot: yet the Subservient Instruments, the lesser Flies could not break throw, but lay entangled in the Cobweb; amongst others Mistress Turner, the first inventress of yellow Starch, was executed in a Cobweb Lawn Ruff of that colour at Tyburn, and with her I believe that yellow Starch, which so much disfigured our Nation, and rendered them so ridiculous and fantastic, will receive its Funeral.[46]

We now come to the reign of Charles I, starting in 1626.

1628 This Summer there was a great Army prepared for forraigne service, whereof the Duke of Buckingham was Generall, who went to Portsmouth, to set all things in readinesse for present dispatch: And upon Saturday the 23. of August, as hee was going thorow his

Hall, which was filled with Commaunders, and strangers, suddainly and vnexpectedly John Felton a Lieutenant, stabd the Duke into the breast, with a knife, and slily withdrew himselfe, undiscerned of any to doe the fact, the Duke stepping to lay hold on him, drew out the knife and began to stagger, the bloud gashing out at his mouth, at which dreadfull sight, certaine Commanders with their strength held him up, the Duke being deprived of speech and life. And then all the doores and passages being stopped, and many with their weapons drawne to kill the Murtherer, the offender himselfe seeing the uproare, boldly confessed, saying, I am the man that did it, and being examined by the Lords, was committed. The King at that time was but six miles from Portsmouth: The Corpes was brought to London, on Saturday the 30. of August, the Nobility, Friends, and Officers brought the Corpes by night with Torches lighted to Wallingford house neere Charing-Crosse: the Murtherer was brought to the Tower the 5 of September. Thursday the 27 of November, the aforenamed John Felton, was brought from the Tower, and Arraigned at the Kings Bench, where he very penitently confessed the fact, saying, I have slaine a most Noble loyall Subiect, and wish that this my right hand might be here cut off, as a true testimony of my hearty sorrow, and had his Judgement to be hanged: from thence he was sent to the Gate-house, where he remained till Saturday, and then sent to Tibourne, and there executed, where hee humbly and heartily repented his offence, and asked forgivenesse of God, the King, and the Dutchesse, and of all the Land, saying, he had slaine a most Noble loyall Subject, and desired all men do pray for him. The next day being Sunday, his Body was sent by Coach towards Portsmouth, and was there hanged in Chaines.[47]

Only one or two priests were executed in England during the first fifteen years of Charles's reign. Between 1641 and 1651 the following priests were drawn, hanged, and quartered at Tyburn merely for being priests. No other charge was made against them, but this sufficed:

Charles had more than one contest with the Parliament on the subject of the execution of priests. In January 1641, Thomas Goodman, a priest and Jesuit, had been condemned. The king reprieved him; the two Houses remonstrated and urged that the law might be executed. Charles reminded Parliament of the inconvenience which might ensue to Protestant Englishmen and others abroad, but having said this he left the final decision to the Houses. Goodman petitioned the king: 'He would esteem his blood well shed to cement the breach between your majesty and your subjects.' He was suffered to die in Newgate. Much the same happened later in the year. Seven priests were condemned on 8 December. The French ambassador exerted himself on their behalf. Charles consulted the two Houses as to a reprieve, to be followed by banishment. He did in fact reprieve them. The Houses petitioned for execution. Charles replied that he desired to banish the priests, 'but if you think the execution of these persons so very necessary to the great and pious work of reformation, we refer it wholly to you, declaring hereby that upon such your resolution signified to the ministers of justice, our warrant for their reprieve is determined, and the law to have its course.' These also were suffered to linger out their lives in Newgate.[48]

In the Thomasson collection of Tracts in the British Museum is one bearing the following title: 'A true and perfect Relation of the Tryall, Condemning, and executing of the 24 Prisoners, who suffered for severall Robberies and Burglaries at Tyburn on Fryday last, which was the 29 of this instant June, 1649.' The names of the criminals are given, twenty-three men and one woman. The prisoners were tied in eight carts, the sexton of St Sepulchre's made his official speech to the culprits, 'which being ended the carts were drave unto Tiburne the Fatall place of execution, where William Lowen the new Hangman fastned eight of them unto each Triangle'. It would seem that there was nothing unusual, nothing to attract attention, in the number executed.

1654 John Southworth, a priest, was sent on the English mission in 1619. He escaped imprisonment till 1627, when he was tried at Lancaster, condemned, reprieved in 1630, and given over to the French ambassador for transportation beyond seas. If he was sent abroad, which seems uncertain, he was soon back, and after a long interval was again arrested, and once more released. He was finally apprehended in 1654. On his arraignment he pleaded that he was not guilty of treason, but in spite of persuasion acknowledged that he was a priest. The court, with, it is said, great reluctance, passed the inevitable sentence. On 28 June five coiners were drawn, hanged, and quartered with Father Southworth. Father Southworth was an old man of 72; nothing was alleged against him but that he was a priest, that he was 'a dangerous seducer'. The guilt of this judicial murder rests wholly with Cromwell. The life of Southworth was in his hands; he was deaf to the suit of the French and Spanish ambassadors for Southworth's life.[49] No more Catholics were executed in England till the Popish Plot broke out in 1678.

Cromwell died in 1658 and despite promises of leniency from the restored Charles II, terrible vengeance followed:

1660 Between 13 and 17 October eight of the Regicides were executed 'at the Round or railed Place neer Charing Crosse'. 'And now the stench of their burnt bowels had so putrified the air, as the inhabitants thereabout petitioned His Majesty there might be no more executed in that place. Therefore on Friday [October 19], Francis Hacker, without remorse, and Daniell Axtell, who dissolved himself into tears and prayers for the King and his own soul, were executed at Tyburn, where Hacker was only hanged, and his brother Rowland Hacker had his body entire, which he begged, and Axtell was quartered.' To finish with the story of the regicides: Colonel Okey, Colonel Barkstead, and Miles Corbet were basely betrayed by Downing, who had been chaplain in Okey's regiment; the States General, in violation of their fundamental maxim to receive and protect those who took refuge in their territory, basely surrendered them. They were executed at Tyburn on April 16, 1662.

A miserable vengeance was wreaked on the dead on the 'carcases' of Cromwell, Ireton, and Bradshaw: December 4. A resolution was passed in the House of Commons; the Lords made an addition, and finally the Resolution stood thus: 'December 8 Resolved, by the Lords and Commons assembled in Parliament, That the carcases of Oliver Cromwell, Henry Ireton, John Bradshaw, Thomas Pride, whether buried in Westminster Abbey or elsewhere, be, with all expedition, taken up and drawn upon a hurdle to Tyburn, and there hanged up in their coffins for some time: and after that buried under the said gallows: and that James Norfolke Esquire, Serjeant at Arms attending the House of Commons, do take care, that this order be put in effectual execution by the common executioner for the County of Middlesex, and all such others to whom it shall respectively appertain: who are required in their several places to conform to and observe this order, with effect; And the Sheriff of Middlesex is to

1 The plaque lies on a traffic island at the junction of two Roman Roads, the Edgware Road and Bayswater Road. It is said to mark the location of the gallows, but there is some dispute as to their exact location.

Above: 2. A near-contemporary illustration of the execution on 24 November 1326, in Hereford, of Hugh Despenser who was sentenced to be disembowelled. Despenser was dragged behind four horses to his place of execution. A fire was lit. He was stripped naked, and hanged from a 50-foot-high gallows and then cut down before he could die. Despenser was then tied to a ladder, and whilst still living had his genitals sliced off and burned: his entrails were slowly pulled out, and, finally, his heart cut out and thrown into the fire. It is reported that he let out a 'ghastly inhuman howl', much to the delight and merriment of the spectators. (Froissart)

Right: 3. A graphic Elizabethan illustration of the process of hanging, drawing and quartering at Tyburn. The victim was usually kept alive for most of the process. One victim is recorded as sitting up and punching the executioner during the latter part of the process.

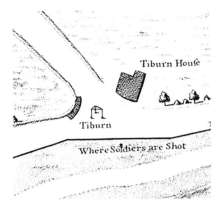

Above: 5. The Tyburn gallows: a detail from the 1746 Rocque map of London. The gallows are shown as standing at the junction of the Edgware Road, and present-day Bayswater Road.

Top left: 4. William de Marisco, an outlaw, was captured in 1242 on the island of Lundy, and on Henry III's order tried, and then dragged from Westminster to be executed by being hanged, drawn and quartered. His corpse was disembowelled and his entrails burnt. His body was then quartered. *Above*: 6. The Tyburn gallows from the 1746 Rocque map, with surrounding area. It can be seen how rural this part of London still was.

7. An illustration of the triple tree and execution process dating from 1680. A clergyman is standing on the cart preaching to the condemned. The horses are waiting to pull the cart away, and the coffin awaits on the cart next to the gallows. Up to eight souls could be hanged at once from each beam.

Below: 8. An early illustration of Connaught Place. The gallows were in the immediate vicinity. An inhabitant from the 1820s commented that he recollected a low house standing at the corner of the Uxbridge Road, close to No. 1, Connaught Place (Arklow House), and that, on the removal of this house, quantities of human bones were found. *Right*: 9. Tyburn in 1750 was still outside the main population area that grew up at the beginning of the nineteenth century. Note the spectator stand where seats were sold to view executions.

Vitæ norma decens pariter mors iunxerit Vna,
Hac duo Thesea pectora nexa fide.

N. bae. f.

10. The Tyburn Turnpike in 1812, looking down what is present-day Oxford Street. The gallows and burial site were in the immediate location of the turnpike.

Above left: 11. The same view of where the Tyburn Turnpike stood, in modern times. Somewhere in the immediate vicinity of the former turnpike are supposed to lie the remains of the regicides Bradshaw, Ireton and Cromwell, which were taken from their graves after the Restoration and buried under the gallows. *Above right*: 12. Executed 1 July 1681, Oliver Plunket was the last of the Roman Catholic martyrs to die in England. Hanged, drawn and quartered at Tyburn, his body was initially buried in two tin boxes next to Jesuits who had died before in the courtyard of St Giles. Exhumed in 1683, after much travelling the head came to rest at Drogheda where, since 29 June 1921, it has rested in Saint Peter's church.

CITY OF WESTMINSTER

105
CATHOLIC MARTYRS
LOST THEIR LIVES
AT THE
TYBURN GALLOWS
NEAR THIS SITE
1535-1681

THE FRIENDS OF TYBURN 1998

TYBURN TREE

THE CIRCULAR STONE ON THE TRAFFIC ISLAND
OO PACES EAST OF THIS POINT MARKS THE SIT
F THE ANCIENT GALLOWS KNOWN AS TYBURN TR
IT WAS DEMOLISHED IN 1759

13. The plaque on the nearby convent in Bayswater Road Road is dedicated to the Catholics executed 300 yards away at Tyburn between 1535 and 1681.

Left: 14. The placard stands in the middle of the Marble Arch roundabout and details in brief the history of the gallows which stood nearby. *Above:* 15. The execution of Earl Ferrers in May 1760. Ferrers, who was probably mentally unbalanced, was executed for the murder of his servant. The earl rejected the mourning coach provided by his friends, and obtained permission to make the journey from the Tower to Tyburn in his own landau, drawn by six horses. He was dressed in a suit of light-coloured clothes, embroidered with silver, said to be his wedding suit.

Dr Cameron drawn on a Sledge to Tyburn

Above left: 16. Earl Ferrers was dissected after execution. 'The body was publicly exposed in a room for three days, and then given up to friends. There exists an engraving showing the body as exposed in the coffin.' *Above right*: 17. Dr Cameron was, on 7 June 1753, hanged and drawn for being involved in the Scottish rebellion of 1745. 'He was suffered to hang for twenty minutes, so that the burning of his bowels was done before eyes closed in death.' Dr Cameron, we are told, 'met death, not so much with fortitude, which implies, in a way, an effort, as with perfect equanimity.'

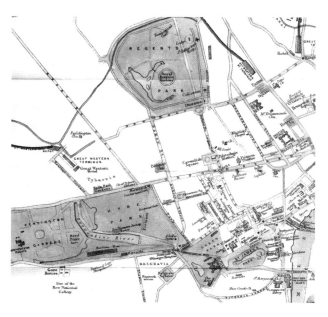

18. Detail from an 1868 map of London showing the district of Tyburnia (centre, lower left) and the development of the area.

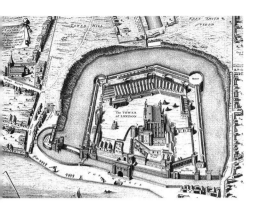

Above: 19. A detail from a 1597 map of the Tower of London shows the site of execution in the top-left part of the map on Tower Hill. *Right*: 20. From 1305 to 1660 the heads of traitors were displayed on spikes at the southern end of old London Bridge on the southern gatehouse. The drawing dates from *c.* 1550.

21. Whilst it was common to display the heads of traitors on London Bridge, the church at the northern end of the bridge, St Magnus the Martyr, was the scene of a number of executions. After the Wyatt rebellion, gallows were set up in a number of places including one at St Magnus church.

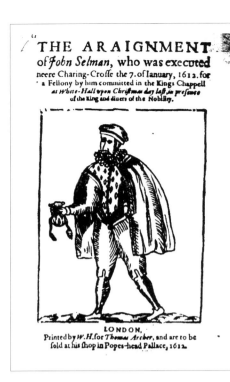

Left: 22. John Selman was executed near Charing Cross on 7 January 1612 for 'a Felony by him committed in the Kings Chapel at White-Hall upon Christmas day last, in presence of the King and divers of the Nobility'. The woodcut of John Selman holding a purse also dates from 1612. *Above*: 23. Tower Green. A modern memorial marks the site where the scaffold is supposed to have stood, but its exact location is not really known. The scaffold was built for each execution, of which there were only seven between 1483 and 1601. In the background is St Peter ad Vincula, where many of the victims were buried.

24. The execution of the son of Charles II, the Duke of Monmouth, on Tower Hill. He rebelled against his uncle, James II. The executioner suffered from stage fright and took five strokes of the axe to remove his head. The executioner was said to be so agitated that he 'was more agitated than he who was to suffer'.

Above right: 25. The plaque on Tower Hill which commemorates the executions of Lord Balmarino and Lord Kilmarnock after the Jacobite Rebellion in 1745. *Centre*: 26. The execution of Lords Balmarino and Kilmarnock on Tower Hill. Kilmarnock, visibly shaken at the sight of his own coffin, prayed for six minutes whilst on the block, leading Walpole to comment that he showed a 'visible unwillingness to depart'. *Below*: 27. The site of the scaffold on Tower Hill is now a memorial garden with a series of plaques for those executed there.

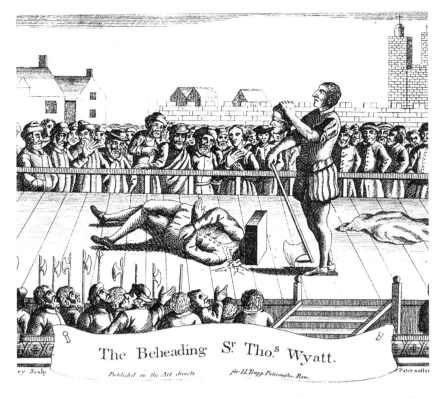

The Beheading Sr Tho.s Wyatt.

ry Sculp   *Published as the Act directs*   *for H.Trapp Paternoster Row.*   *Pater noster*

28. The execution of Sir Thomas Wyatt on Tower Hill in 1554 for his uprising against Mary I. His body was quartered, his head placed on a stake near St James's and reportedly stolen after ten days.

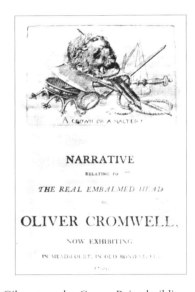

Above left: 29. The Angel, formerly The Bowl in St Giles, near the Centre Point building in Charing Cross Road. The procession passed by here from Newgate to Tyburn. The condemned stopped here for refreshments on their way to the gallows. *Above right*: 30. An advertisement dating from 1799 to see Oliver Cromwell's head. His exhumed body was buried next to the Tyburn gallows, and his head placed above Westminster Hall. In 1685 it blew down, was rescued, and became an exhibit before being finally buried in the grounds of his old college, Sidney Sussex College, Cambridge, in 1960.

Above: 31. The route from Newgate to Tyburn, from Rocque's London map of 1746. *Right*: 32. The memorial in the wall of St Bartholomew's Hospital in Smithfield to the Scottish leader William Wallace. He was probably executed at Tyburn, not Smithfield. *Below*: 33. Smithfield. The area where it is likely executions took place. Smithfield was notorious during the reign of Mary I (1553–8), when possibly as many as 278 Protestants were executed for heresy.

34. The burning of four Protestants at Smithfield during the Marian persecution.

35. The new gallows at Newgate. The Tyburn gallows were abolished in 1783. Public executions commenced here in the same year.

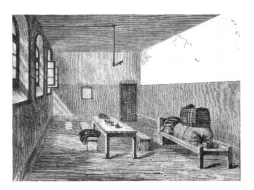

36. The condemned cell in Newgate which Dickens referred to as 'stone dungeons'. The cell would house up to four people at a time.

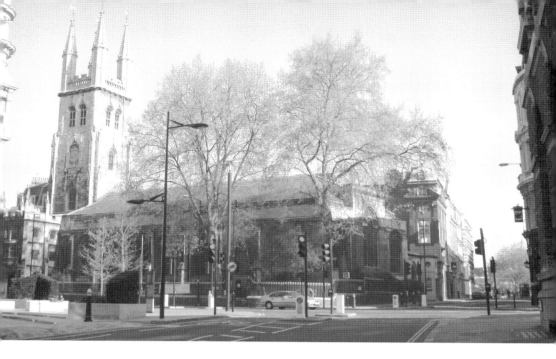

Above: 37. This is the view from the approximate position where the gallows were erected prior to executions. The bell would be rung to mark the execution. Still on display in a glass case is the handbell rung outside of the condemned man's cell the midnight before execution. *Right*: 38. An execution in front of Newgate in 1863 with St Sepulchre visible in the distance.

39. The 'burning, plundering and destruction' of Newgate Prison. This engraving was made a year after the riots. Prisoners were released, and taken to blacksmiths to have their chains removed.

40. The Obelisk, a mile south of Blackfriar's Bridge, marks the gathering area of Gordon and his petitioners in what was then St George's Fields. Here also were some rioters executed after the troubles had ceased.

Above: 41. Here, near the north-east part of Bloomsbury Square, John Gray, Charles Kent and Letitia Holland were executed for being party to setting fire to the mansion of Lord Chief Justice Mansfield. *Right*: 42. Cheapside. Honey Lane, where the 'Standard' stood. Just over the road is Bow church. It was here that executions took place, including those carried out by Wat Tyler and later Jack Cade.

Above right: 43. Cheapside in the seventeenth century. Executions took place in the immediate vicinity of the Eleanor Cross. The cross was demolished by order of Parliament in May 1643 as being associated with idolatry. *Below*: 44. The Braun and Hogenberg map of London, which was published in 1572 shows the gallows, centre picture, at Charing Cross. *Centre*: 45. Old Palace Yard. The best known personages to die at these places are the Gunpowder Plot conspirators, who were executed within a day of each other in the January of 1606, four at St Paul's Churchyard, and four at Old Palace Yard, Westminster. Sir Walter Raleigh was executed here in 1618 after many years of imprisonment in the Tower. Old Palace Yard is situated opposite the St Stephens entrance to Parliament.

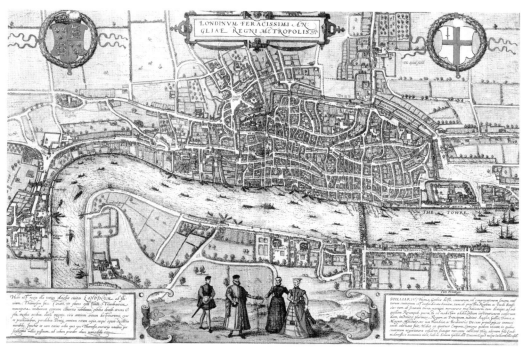

Below: 46. Raleigh's execution at Old Palace Yard. Asking to see the axe, Raleigh ran his fingers along the blade and commented to the sheriff that the axe 'tis a sharp medicine, but a sound cure for all diseases'. *Above*: 47. New Palace Yard. After the execution of Charles I, some of his commanders and supporters were captured, tried and executed. The Duke of Hamilton, Earl of Holland, and Arthur, Lord Capel were executed on a scaffold 'over against the great hall gate, in the site of the place where the high court of justice formerly sat, the hall doors being open…' All three died on the same day, 9 March 1649. *Left*: 48. The bronze horse with Charles I on horseback at the southern end of Trafalgar Square looks down Whitehall to the place where the king was executed. It was at this exact spot, where the statue was placed in 1675, that Charles II attended to watch the execution of some of the regicides.

Above left: 49. Execution Dock Wapping lies between Wapping Old and Wapping New Stairs, about a mile west of the Tower of London. Probably the most famous execution to take place here was that of the pirate Captain Kidd on 23 May 1701.
Above right: 50. The modern-day view from the Captain Kidd pub. Comparing the previous illustration suggests that the gallows stood by Wapping New Stairs.

51. Wapping foreshore and the Captain Kidd pub. It is likely that the gallows were located in the immediate vicinity of the where the pub now stands.

52. St Mark's church, Kennington stands on the site of the gallows which stood opposite today's Oval tube station. Between 1678 and 1799, 129 executions took place here.

Above left: 53. The Methodist preacher George Whitfield at the Kennington gibbet *c.* 1748.
Above right: 54. Rocque's map of 1746 showing the location of Kennington Common and the gallows.

56. Hounslow Heath, now a hidden but well-preserved nature reserve, played host to a number of gibbets where highwaymen were hanged as a warning to others. The Three Magpies pub on the A4, Bath Road situated on the Heathrow perimeter was near the site of a nineteenth century murder and subsequent execution.

Above: 55. Lincoln's Inn Fields bandstand. It was in the vicinity of the modern bandstand that an inscription once marked the place of execution of Lord Russell in 1683. It read: 'On this spot was beheaded, William, Lord Russell, a lover of constitutional liberty 21st July, AD 1683.' The executioner took four blows with the axe to decapitate Russell. *Right*: 57. St Paul's Churchyard was a common place of execution including four of those involved in the Gunpowder Plot of 1605. Executions took place 'upon the spot called London House Yard, now a passage from St Paul's Churchyard to Paternoster Row'. Thus the gallows stood in the immediate vicinity of St Paul's Cross.

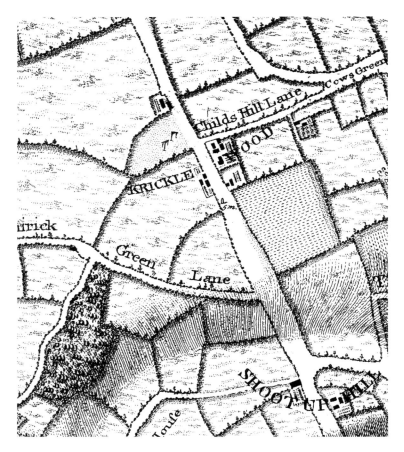

58. The Rocque 1746 map shows a double gibbet and a gallows on the corner of Cricklewood Broadway and the present day Chichele Road. The gallows stood in modern-day terms where Oaklands Road meets the Edgware Road, Cricklewood Broadway.

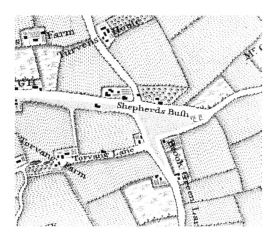

Above left: 59. Rocque's 1746 map shows gallows and gibbet at the eastern end of Shepherd's Bush Green. *The Gentleman's Magazine* in 1856 comments that 'there were gallows and occasional executions at Shepherd's Bush, when Tybourn succeeded St Giles'. *Above right*: 60. The River Thames was lined with gibbets as a warning to those arriving by river. The Rocque map of 1746 shows a gibbet situated at the southern end of the Isle of Dogs. A highly visible location.

give his assistance herein, as there shall be occasion: And the Dean of Westminster is desired to give directions to his officers of the Abbey to be assistant in the execution of this order.' A new gallows had been erected for the purpose.[50]

1660 On 9 June the House of Commons resumed debate on the Act of General Pardon, Indemnity, and Oblivion, and a list was produced of some who, though they did not sit at the trial of Charles I on 27 January 1648, did sit on some of the preceding days. The subject was considered on subsequent occasions, and finally an Act was passed (1661), enacting that Lord Monson, Sir Henry Mildmay, and Robert Wallop (and others who had fled) should on January 27 1662, be 'carried to the Tower of London and from thence drawne upon Sledges with Ropes about theire necks, and according to the manner of persons executed for High Treason quite through the streets of London unto the Gallows att Tiburn', and then carried back in like manner to the Tower or such other prison as the king may think fit, and remain prisoners during their lives. Accordingly on 27 January 1662: 'This morning, going to take water, upon Tower-hill we met with three sleddes standing there to carry my Lord Monson and Sir H. Mildmay and another to the gallows and back again, with ropes about their necks: which is to be repeated every year, this being the day of their sentencing the king.'

The diarist John Evelyn tells us that on 30 January 1661:

> The odious carcasses of O. Cromwell, H. Ireton, and J. Bradshaw drawn upon sledges to Tyburn, and being pull'd out of their Coffins, there hang'd at the severall Angles of that Triple-tree till Sunset. Then taken down, beheaded, and their loathsome Truncks thrown into a deep hole under the Gallowes. Their heads were afterwards set upon Poles on the top of Westminster Hall. Here Pepys saw them.

1661 This year witnessed the outbreak of the Fifth Monarchy men. John James, a small-coal man, was executed at Tyburn. 'The sheriff and hangman were so civil to him in his execution, as to suffer him to be dead before he was cut down, beheaded, bowelled, and quartered. His quarters were set on the gates of the City, his head was first fixed on London Bridge, but afterwards upon a pole, near Bulstake Alley, Whitechapel, in which was James's meeting-house.'

1662, December 22 Thomas Tonge, George Phillips, Francis Stubbs and Nathaniel Gibbs, convicted of taking part in a plot to seize the Tower and Whitehall, to kill the King and declare a Commonwealth. They were drawn to Tyburn on two hurdles, hanged, beheaded and quartered; their heads were set up on poles on Tower Hill.

1670 In February of this year ended the brilliant career of Claude Duval, the famous highwayman. There had been highwaymen before Duval, as he was succeeded by others. But the great merit of Duval is that he gave a tone and dignity to the profession which it never wholly lost. He was born in Normandy, and came over to England as page to the Duke of Richmond: 'after he had hanged a convenient time, he was cut down, and, by persons well dressed, carried into a mourning-coach, and so conveyed to the Tangier-tavern in St Giles, where he lay in state all that night, the room hung with black cloth, the hearse covered with escutcheons, eight wax-tapers burning, and as many tall gentlemen with long black cloakes attending; mum was the word, great silence expected from all that visited, for fear of disturbing this sleeping lion. And this ceremony had lasted much longer, had not one of the judges (whose name I must not mention here, lest he should incur the displeasure of the ladies) sent to disturb this pageantry.'

1677 Thomas Sadler is said to have been in prison fifteen times before he planned his last and greatest exploit. With the aid of two accomplices, he stole from Great Queen Street, the Lord Chancellor's mace and purse (the official purse, one of the emblems of the office). Sadler was so delighted with his success, that in crossing Lincoln's Inn Fields he made one of the confederates precede him with the mace on his shoulder, while he himself strutted behind him, followed by the purse-bearer. They bore their plunder to a house in the City, where it was locked up in a cupboard. Curiosity led a maid to look through a chink in the door, when to her wonderment she saw what she took to be the King's crown. This led to the discovery of the robbery. On his trial Sadler behaved with superb frankness. 'My lord,' he said, addressing the court, 'I own the fact, and it was I and this man [pointing to one that stood by him at the bar] that robbed my Lord Chancellor: and the three others are clear of the fact, though I cannot say but they were confederates with us in the concealment of the prize after it was taken. This I declare,' said he, 'to the honourable bench, that I may be clear of the blood of these other three persons.' However, the court went on in a legal way, and another witness began to demonstrate in what manner he was taken: to whom the prisoner answered in this manner: 'prithee, fellow, do not make such a long narration of my being taken; thou seest I am here, and I own that I and this man, as aforesaid, are guilty of the fact.' It seems that one of the confederates was reprieved. Sadler and Johnson, one of his companions, were among the five men executed at Tyburn on 16 March 1677.[51]

1683 In this year we have the executions for the Rye House Plot, the object of which was to capture Charles II on his return from Newmarket. 'July 20. Capt. Thomas Walcott, John Rouse, and William Hone, were drawn, about 9 in the morning, upon sledges, the two last in one, and the 1st by himself, to Tyburn, and there hanged and quartered, according to the sentence past on them on the 14th at the Old Bailey, for the late conspiracy. July 21. The quarters of Walcot, Hone, and Rouse are buried, but their heads are sett on these places.'[52] William, Lord Russell was executed in Lincoln's Inn Fields on 21 July 1683.

1684 Sir Thomas Armstrong was concerned in the Rye House Plot, but had fled to Holland and was outlawed. He was taken at Leyden by order of the States, brought to England, and committed to Newgate. Brought to the King's Bench bar, he was refused trial, and sentence of death was passed upon him as an outlaw: 'The 20th June, Sir Thomas Armstrong was drawn upon a sledge, with a very numerous guard to Tyburn; where being come, Dr Tenison prayed with him, who seemed very penitent: he prayed himself also very fervently; which done, he delivered a paper to the sheriffs, and submitted himself to the sentence: after he had hang'd about half an hour he was taken down, and quartered according to his sentence, and his quarters were brought back in the sledge to Newgate ... Sir Thomas Armstrong's quarters are disposed off: a forequarter is sett on Temple bar, his head on Westminster, another quarter is sent down to the town of Stafford, for which he was a Parliament man. The head was taken down after the Revolution.'[53]

We now enter on the short and troubled reign of James II.

1685 James Burton was outlawed for having taken part in the Rye House Plot (1683). Elizabeth Gaunt, a poor woman, gave him shelter and finally got him a passage to Holland. Burton returned, took part in Monmouth's rebellion in 1685, and after Monmouth's defeat again sought refuge in London. At the entreaty of his wife, Fernley, a barber, a neighbour of Mrs Gaunt, gave him shelter. To save his own neck Burton gave information against his benefactors for protecting him. He was not ashamed to appear in court against them, and the Crown lawyers were not ashamed to produce his evidence. Fernley was hanged at Tyburn, Elizabeth Gaunt was burnt in the same place on 23 October 1685. In prison she wrote her Last Speech. She says, 'I did but relieve an unworthy, poor, distressed family, & lo I must dye for it; well, I desire in the Lamb-like nature of the Gospell to forgive all that are concerned, & to say, Lord, lay it not to their charge; but I fear it will not; nay I believe, when he comes to make inquisition for blood, it will be found at the door of the furious Judge ... my blood will also be found at the door of the unrighteous Jury, who found me guilty upon the single oath of an out-lawd man.' 'Pen, the quaker,' says Burnet, 'told me, he saw her die. She laid the straw about her for burning her speedily; and behaved herself in such a manner, that all the spectators melted in tears' (Burnet, *Hist. of his Own Time*, i. 649). 'Since that terrible day,' writes Macaulay, 'no woman has suffered death in England for any political offence.' This is true only if we except the cases in which women were burnt as guilty of treason for coining. It was by a narrow chance that Mrs Gaunt was the last. On 19 January 1693, Mrs Merryweather was sentenced to be burnt for printing treasonable pamphlets, but, after being more than once reprieved, was pardoned on 23 February (Luttrell).

1686 May 20–22 Sessions at Old Bailey, when 16 received sentence of death. The 28th, five men of those lately condemned at the Sessions were executed at Tyburn; one of them was Pascha Rose, the new hangman, so that now Ketch is restored to his place.[54]

1686 On the night of April 12 two of his Majesty's mails from Holland were robbed, near Ilford, of 5,000 in gold, belonging to some Jews in London. Richard Alborough, Oliver Hawley, and John Condom were indicted for the robbery. Alborough pleading guilty was sentenced to death, & the same sentence was passed on the others after trial. July the 2nd, Oliver Hawley and John Condom were executed at Tyburn.

Here is a strange incident: at the Sessions at the Old Bailey held on

13–16 October fourteen persons received sentence of death. 'Edward Skelton, one of the criminalls that received sentence of death this last sessions at the Old Baily, has been beg'd of the King by 18 maids clothed in white, and since is married to one of them in the Presse yard.'[55]

1690 September 12 6 persons were executed at Tyburn; some of them behaved themselves very impudently, calling for sack, and drank king James's health, and affronted the ordinary at the gallows, and refused his assistance; and bid the people return to their obedience and send for king James back.[56]

1690 In this year occurred a famous case of stealing an heiress. This was made a felony by Henry VII (1487). We will let Luttrell tell the story of the abduction and its result, day by day: 'November 7. One Mrs Mary Wharton, a young heiresse of about 1500 per ann., and about 13 years of age, comeing home with her aunt, Mrs Byerley, in their coach about 9 at night, and alighting out of it at her own aunt, was violently seized on and putt into a coach and 6 horses and carried away. November 15. Mrs Wharton, who was lately stole, is returned home to her friends, having been married against her consent to Captain Campbell [brother to Lord Argyle] ... A proclamation hath been published by their majesties for the discovering and apprehending captain James Campbell, Archibald Montgomery, and sir John Jonston, for stealing away Mrs Wharton. [The proclamation included 'divers others'.] November 25. Sir John Jonston, concerned in the stealing of Mrs Wharton, is taken and committed to Newgate. December 10. The sessions began at the Old Bailey, and held the 11th, 12th, 13th, and 14th dayes of this month, where 22 persons received sentence of death (and among them sir John Jonston, for stealing Mrs Wharton), 9 were burnt in the hand, 1 ordered to be transported, and 6 sentenced to be whipt. December 18. Intercession has been made to his majestie on the behalf of sir John Jonston, lately condemned, for his pardon; which he hath denied unlesse it be desired by the friends of Mrs Wharton. December 23. Sir John Jonston, condemned for stealing Mrs Wharton, went up in a mourning coach to Tyburn, and was executed for the same; and his body was delivered to his friends, in order to it's being buried.'[57]

1690 December 22 Thirteen persons were executed at Tyburn for several crimes; also a woman at Newgate for setting the prison on fire; and also a notorious highway man, commonly called the Golden Farmer [this was William Davis, known by this title], was executed in Fleetstreet, at the end of Salisbury court, and is after to be hang'd in chains upon Bagshott heath.[58]

1692 September 22 Information is given of near 300 coyners and clippers dispersed in divers parts of this citty, on which warrants are out against severall; one from the lords of the treasury, another by the cheife justice, and a *3d* by the masters of the mint.

1692 Towards the end of the year Luttrell has several entries in his diary relating to a celebrated highwayman, 'captain' James Whitney: 'December. Witney, the notorious highway man, offers to bring in 80 stout men of his gang to the kings service, if he may have his pardon. December 6. This morning his majestie sent a party of horse to look after Whitney, the great highwayman, on some notice he was lurking between Barnet and St Albans: they mett with him at the first of the said towns, who finding himselfe attackt, made his defence and killed one of them, and wounded some others: but at last was taken and brought to London. His majestie was very glad he was taken, being a great ringleader of that crew.' This must have been a mistake, as shown by the following entries: 'December 20. The lords C. and B. were on Satturday last to meet Whitney, a great highwayman, on honour; he offers to bring in 30 horse, with as many stout men, to serve the king, provided he may have his pardon, and will give a summe of money besides: but the issue thereof not known.'

1693, January 6 On Satturday last Whitney, the famous highwayman, was taken without Bishopsgate; he was discovered by one Hill as he walkt the street, who observed where he housed, then, calling some assistance, he went to the door; but Whitney defended himselfe for an hour, but the people encreasing, and the officers of Newgate being sent for, he surrendered himselfe, but had before stabb'd the said Hill with a bayonet, but not mortall: he was cuff'd and shackled with irons and committed to Newgate; and on Sunday 2 more of his gang were also seized and committed; one kept a livery stable in Moor fields. January 7. Strongly reported yesterday that Whitney had made his escape out of Newgate, but he continues closely confined there, and has 40 pound weight of iron on his leggs; he had his taylor make him a rich embroidered suit, with perug and hatt … but the keeper refused to let him wear them, because they would disguise him from being known. On the 8th five of Whitney's gang apprehended but 2 of them escaped.

1693 January 28 At the Old Baily sessions '8 highwaymen received sentence of death, Whitney, Grasse, Fetherstone, Nedland, Poor, Holland and 2 more'. Yesterday 9 persons were carried to Tyburn, where 8 were executed, 7 hyghwaymen, and one for clipping; Whitney was brought back, having a reprieve for 10 dayes, and was brought back to Newgate with a rope about his neck, a vast crowd of people following him. Last night Whitney was carried in a sedan to Whitehall and examined; 'tis said he discovers who hired the persons to rob the mailes so often. Whitney, 'tis said, has been examined upon a design to kill the King. Whitney, 'tis said, will be executed next week; others say his reprieve is grounded on the discovery of his accomplices, with their houses of reception, and way of living.

1693 February 2 Yesterday being the 1st instant, capt. James Whitney, highwayman, was executed at Porter's block, near Cow crosse in Smithfield; he seemed to dye very penitent; was an hour and halfe in the cart before turn'd off. Luttrell mentions that in January there were near 20 highwaymen in Newgate.

1694 July 19 Yesterday 9 men and 3 women were executed at Tyburn; amongst them was Wilkinson the goldsmith, with several others for clipping; one Paynes, convicted for murder, who by the confession of one of his accomplices has killed 5 or 6 persons in a short time; he kickt the ordinary out of the cart at Tyburn, and pulled off his shoes, sayeing, hee'd contradict the old proverb, and not dye in them.[59]

1695 At the Old Bailey Sessions: July 6. Mr Moor, the rich tripeman of Westminster, was found guilty of clipping and coyning; and some others will be tried for the like offence July 13. Yesterday four men were executed at Tyburn, three of them for clipping, one of which was John Moore, the tripeman, said to have gott a good estate by clipping, and to have offered 6000 l. for his pardon (Luttrell, iii. 497). July 16. Moor the tripeman being hang'd for clipping, the duke of Somerset has seized upon his house, worth 1000 l, being within his mannor of Isleworth. This day a rich chandler of Lambeth and a house-keeper in Long Acre were seized for clipping.[60]

In February, 1696, came to a head 'the Assassination Plot', the most dangerous of all the Plots formed against William III. The

King was, according to custom, to go to hunt in Richmond Park on
15 February. Advantage was to be taken of this to assassinate him.
For some reason he did not go, and the execution of the scheme was
deferred. But meanwhile one of the conspirators gave information
to the Government. Numerous arrests were made, followed by trials
and executions. On 18 March Robert Charnock, Edward King,
and Thomas Keys were executed at Tyburn. They were followed on
3 April by Sir John Friend and Sir William Perkins. The populace
of London flocked to Tyburn in numbers exceeding all precedent to
witness the execution of Friend, found guilty by the Court of high
treason, and by the people of a crime that touched them more nearly
the brewing of execrable beer. Three non-juring divines attended the
condemned men to the scaffold, Jeremy Collier, and two of less note,
Shadrach Cook and William Snatt, who absolved the criminals 'in a
manner more than ordinarily practised in the Church of England'.
For this Cook and Snatt were committed to Newgate. Macaulay
says that they were not brought to trial. It appears, however, that
they were actually indicted, and found guilty of high crimes and
misdemeanours (Luttrell, iv. 80) and imprisoned for a short time.
Collier kept out of the way, and was in consequence outlawed,
remaining under the sentence to the end of his days. Numerous
tracts were written on the subject. On 29 April Brigadier Rookwood,
Charles Cranburne, and Major Lowick were executed at Tyburn,
they also having been condemned for the Plot. This completes the
story of the executions at Tyburn for the Assassination Plot.

1697, July 20 The 16th past, 14 malefactors were executed at
Tyburn; 3 men and 1 woman for coining, 2 men for counterfeiting
stamp't paper, a woman for murthering her bastard child; and 7 more
for robbery and burglary; and the French woman, who murdered
Mrs Pullein, was hanged at the end of Suffolk Street, where the fact
was committed. November 4. Yesterday 6 persons were executed at
Tyburn; two for coining, one for robbing on the high way, and 3 for
counterfeiting stampt paper, of which Mr Salisbury the minister was
one; he had the favour to goe to Tyburn in a mourning coach, and
his body was brought back in a herse.

Salisbury was a non-juring parson of Sussex; the evidence against
him showed that he did not commit the forgery for want, 'as having
a good estate and a good living, but only to prejudice king William's

Government'. A few days later Luttrell records the committal of another parson for the same offence.

1698, December 22 Yesterday fourteen men and one woman were executed at Tyburn; two of the men were drawn in a sledge, and were for coining; one man was carried in a coach, for robbing on the high way and the rest in carts, for burglary and robbery on the high way; and one for murther. Including these, Luttrell records the execution at Tyburn this year of 62 persons.

1699 Luttrell records the execution this year at Tyburn of 51 persons. 'March 16. Three prisoners were this week taken in the very act of coining in Newgate. April 20. Yesterday, one Larkin, alias Young, with another, were executed at Tyburn; the former for coyning in Newgate.'

1705, December 12 One John Smith, condemned lately at the Old Baily for burglary, was carried to Tyburn to be executed, and was accordingly hanged up, and after he had hung about 7 minutes, a reprieve came, so he was cutt down, and immediately lett blood and put into a warm bed, which, with other applications, brought him to himself again with much adoe.[61]

1716, May 14 Colonel Oxburgh. May 25, Richard Gascoign. July 18, Rev. William Paul and John Hall. In his account of the execution of Paul and Hall, Mr Lorrain, the ordinary of Newgate, says: 'The cart being drawn away, and they being turned off, the People gave a mighty shout, and with loud Acclamations said, God save King George. To which I say, Amen.'

1718, March 17 Execution of Ferdinando Marquis de Palleotti. The Duke of Shrewsbury, being at Rome, fell in love with Palleotti's sister, and upon the lady's conversion to Protestantism, married her. Ferdinando visited his sister in England. He was addicted to gambling, and made such demands upon his sister's purse that at length she refused further supplies. He was arrested for debt, and liberated by her. Walking in the street one day, he ordered his servant to call upon a gentleman in the neighbourhood, and ask for a loan. The servant showing reluctance to fulfil the order, the marquis drew his sword and ran him through the body. According to the ordinary, the marquis thought it a great hardship that he should die for so small a matter as killing his servant James Mountague. A few hours after the execution of the marquis, James Shepherd, an adherent of the Pretender, was drawn to Tyburn and there hanged and quartered.[62]

1718, May 31 The hangman of Tyburn, John Price, known by the common name Jack Ketch, was hanged, for murder, near the scene of the crime, in Bunhill-Fields.

1721, February 8 On this day were executed at Tyburn four men, one of whom had undergone the *peine forte et dure* (crushing torture to force them to plead). Four men were indicted for highway robberies. Two refusing to plead, the court gave orders to read the judgment appointed to be executed on such as stand mute or refuse to plead to their indictment. 'That the prisoner shall be sent to the prison from whence he came, and put into a mean room, stopped from the light, and shall there be laid on the bare ground without any litter, straw, or other covering, and without any garment about him except something about his middle. He shall lie upon his back, his head shall be covered and his feet shall be bare. One of his arms shall be drawn with a cord to the side of the room, and the other arm to the other side, and his legs shall be served in the like manner. Then there shall be laid upon his body as much iron or stone as he can bear, and more. And the first day after he shall have three morsels of barley bread, without any drink, and the second day he shall be allowed to drink as much as he can, at three times, of the water that is next the prison door, except running water, without any bread; and this shall be his diet till he dies: and he against whom the judgment shall be given forfeits his goods to the King.' This having no effect on the prisoners, the executioner (as is usual in such cases) was ordered to tie their thumbs together, and draw the cord as tight as he was able, which was immediately done; neither this, nor all the admonitions of the court being sufficient to bring them to plead, they were sentenced to be pressed to death. They were carried back to Newgate. As soon as they entered the press-room, Phillips desired that he might return to the bar and plead, but Spiggott continuing obstinate was put under the press. He bore three hundred and fifty pounds weight for half an hour, but then fifty more added, he begged that he might be carried back to plead, which favour was granted. After the treatment he was very faint and almost speechless for two days. One of his reasons given to the ordinary of Newgate for enduring the press was that none might reproach his children by telling them their father was hanged. Before he was taken out of the press, he was in a kind of slumber and had hardly any sense of pain left.

1721, July 5 Barbara Spencer was burnt at Tyburn for coining. At the stake 'she was very desirous of praying, and complained of the dirt and stones thrown by the mob behind her, which prevented her thinking sedately on futurity. One time she was quite beat down by them.' [63]

1721, December 22 Nathaniel Hawes, a young man of 20, had been out of prison but a few days when he robbed a man on the highway. He refused to plead, because a handsome suit of clothes had been taken from him, and he was resolved not to go to the gallows in a shabby suit. The court ordered that his thumbs should be tied together. The cord was pulled by two officers till it broke, and this was repeated several times without effect. He was then put in the press, and gave in when he had borne a weight of 250lbs for about seven minutes.

1724, November 16 John, or Jack Sheppard, for burglary. Jack Sheppard does not seem to have committed any crime worse than burglary: his hands were not stained with blood. He was famed for several remarkable escapes. According to Monsieur Cesar de Saussure, who was in England in 1726, the weight was increased every four hours.[64] He had once escaped from Newgate and being again arrested; unusual care was taken of him. But he once more and for the last time escaped, being soon after captured while drunk. For better security he was lodged in a strong room called the Castle, where he was hand-cuffed, loaded with a heavy pair of irons, and chained to a staple in the floor. The Sessions at the Old Bailey began on 14 October, and Jack, knowing that the keepers would be busy in attending the court, thought that this would be the only time to make a push for his liberty. 'The next day, about two in the afternoon, one of the keepers carried Jack his dinner, examined his irons, and found all fast. Jack then went to work. He got off his hand-cuffs, and with a crooked nail he found on the floor, opened the great padlock that fastened his chain to the staple. Next he twisted asunder a small link of the chain between his legs, and drawing up his feet-locks as high as he could, he made them fast with his garters. He attempted to get up the chimney, but had not advanced far before his progress was stopped by an iron bar that went across within-side, and therefore being descended, he went to work on the outside, and with a piece of his broken chain picked out the mortar, and removing a small stone or two about six feet from the floor, he got out the iron bar, an inch square and near a yard long, and this proved of great service to him. He presently made so large a breach that he got into the Red-Room over the Castle, there he found a great nail, which was another very useful implement. The door of his room had not been opened for seven years past; but in less than seven minutes he wrenched off the lock, and got into the entry leading to the Chapel. Here he found a door bolted on the other side, upon which he broke a hole through the wall, and pushed the bolt back. Coming now to the chapel-door, he broke off one of the iron spikes, which he kept for further use, and so got into an entry between the chapel and the lower leads. The door of this entry was very strong, and fastened with a great lock, and what was worse, the night had overtaken him, and he was forced to work in the dark. However, in half an hour, by the help of the great nail, the chapel spike, and the iron bar, he forced off the box of the lock, and opened the door, which led him to another yet more difficult, for it was not only locked, but barred and bolted. When he had tried in vain to make this lock and box give way, he wrenched the fillet from the main post of the door, and the box and staples came off with it: and now St Sepulchre's chimes went eight. There was yet another door betwixt him and the lower leads; but it being only bolted within-side, he opened it easily, and mounting to the top of it, he got over the wall, and so to the upper leads. His next consideration was, how to get down; for which purpose looking round him, and finding the top of the Turner's house adjoining to Newgate, was the most convenient place to alight upon, he resolved to descend thither; but as it would have been a dangerous leap, he went back to the Castle the same way he came, and fetched a blanket he used to lie on. This he made fast to the wall of Newgate, with the spike he stole out of the Chapel, and so sliding down, dropped upon the Turner's leads, and then the clock struck nine. Luckily for him, the Turner's garret-door on the leads happened to be open. He went in, and crept softly down one pair of stairs, when he heard company talking in a room below. His irons giving a clink, a woman started, and said, "Lord! What noise is that?" Somebody answered, "The dog or the cat"; and thereupon Sheppard returned up to the garret, and having continued there above two hours, he ventured down a second time, when he heard a gentleman take leave of the company, and saw the maid light him down stairs. As soon as the maid came back, and had shut the chamber door, he made the best of his way to the street door, unlocked it, and so made his escape about twelve at night.' But on 31 October Jack made merry at a public-house in Newgate Street, with two ladies of his acquaintance, afterwards treated his mother in Clare Market with three quarters of brandy, and in a word got so drunk that he forgot all caution and was once more apprehended. He still had schemes for eluding justice. He had got hold of a penknife; with this on the road to Tyburn he would cut the cords binding his hands, jump from the cart into the crowd and run through Little Turnstile, where the mounted officers could not follow him, and he reckoned on the sympathy of the mob to help him to make good his escape. But he was searched, and the knife was taken from him. He had one last hope; he urged his friends to get possession of his body as soon as cut down, and put it into a warm bed; so he thought, and precedents were not wanting, his life might be prolonged. This, too, came to naught (Villette, i. 261-6). In the twenty-third year of his age he 'died with great difficulty, and much pitied by the mob', the prince of prison-breakers. Villette says: 'I don't remember any felon in this kingdom, whose adventures have made so much noise as Sheppard's.'

1725, May 24 Jonathan Wild, 'the thief-taker'. Jonathan Wild, whose exploits were celebrated by Fielding in *Jonathan Wild, the Great* invented a new method which may be described as running with the hare and riding with the hounds. He was in league with great numbers of thieves of all kinds, from highwaymen downwards. This body was described as 'a corporation of thieves of which Wild was the head or director'. He divided the country into districts, assigning gangs for the working of each. These gangs accounted to him for the proceeds of their robberies. He selected by preference convicts returned from transportation, because, in case of accident, they could not give legal evidence against him; moreover, they were in his power, and if any rebelled he could hang them. For fifteen years he carried on this system. His depredations were on a large scale: he had in his pay several artists to alter watches, rings, and other objects of value, so as not to be recognised by their owners. At his trial he circulated among the jury a list of persons apprehended and convicted by his means: 35 for highway robbery, 22 for burglary, 10 for returning from transportation. It would be too tedious, he said, to give a list of minor cases. On the way to Tyburn he was cursed and pelted. The rest of the batch being tied up, the executioner told Wild he might have any reasonable time to prepare himself. This so incensed the mob that they threatened to knock the hangman on the head if he did not at once perform the duties of his office. The body was buried in the churchyard of Old St Pancras, but was afterwards removed, by surgeons as was supposed.

1726, May 9 Catherine Hays and Thomas Billings, executed for the murder of John Hays, the husband of Catherine. Thomas Wood, also condemned for the murder, died on May 4 in the 'Condemned-Hold'. Hays's body was cut up by the murderers, and the head thrown into the Thames, but it was recovered and set up on a pole in the churchyard of St Margaret's, Westminster. This led to identification and discovery of the criminals. Catherine Hays was drawn on a sledge to Tyburn. Here she was chained to a stake and faggots were piled around her. A rope round her neck was passed through a hole in the stake. When the fire had got well alight and had reached the woman, the executioner pulled the rope, intending to strangle her, but, the fire reaching his hands, he was forced to desist. More faggots were then piled on the woman, and in about three or four hours she was reduced to ashes. Billings was put in irons as he was hanging on the gallows, his body was then cut down, carried to a gibbet about a hundred yards distant, and there suspended in chains.[65]

1732, October 9 Thirteen executed at Tyburn.

1733, January 29 Twelve malefactors, condemned in the three preceding sessions, executed at Tyburn.

1733, May 28 John Davis, feigning sickness, begged that he might not be tied in the cart. When he came to the Tree, he jumped from the cart and ran across two fields. A countyman knocked him down, and he was brought back and hanged.

1733, December 19 Thirteen executed at Tyburn. Among them were a man and a woman condemned for coining. They were, as usual, drawn in a sledge: the man, after being hanged, was slashed across the body. The woman, chained to a stake, was first strangled and then burnt.

1743 At the Old Bailey sessions, 7–12 September, were indicted James Stansbury and Mary his wife, for the robbery of Mr or Captain George Morgan. The case is very interesting, as having furnished to Hogarth the motive of one of his prints in the series of *The Effects of Industry and Idleness*. Captain Morgan, going home in the early hours of the morning of 17 July, seeing a lady in the street, feared for her safety, and gallantly offered to escort her home. He was taken into a house where he was robbed and assaulted. The house, in Hanging-Sword Alley, Fleet Street, bore an execrable reputation, in virtue of which it was known as 'Blood-Bowl House'. At the trial Mary Stansbury asked a witness, 'Have I not let you go all over the house, to see if there were any trapdoors as it was represented?' The witness, Sharrock, replied that he had looked all over the house and saw no trap-door. It will be recollected that in Hogarth's print the body of a murdered man is being thrust through a trap-door. The same witness spoke of the house as 'Blood-Bowl House'. Stansbury asked him how he came to know of the Blood Bowl, to which Sharrock replied that he had seen it in the newspapers. (I have been less fortunate: I have not found accounts in contemporary newspapers referring to the name or to the trap-door). Stansbury was acquitted: his wife was sentenced to death, the sentence being afterwards commuted to one of transportation. Stansbury was afterwards convicted of burglary. He described himself as a clockmaker, living in Whitechapel, from which we may infer that Hanging-Sword Alley had become too hot for him. It would seem too that he had not retired from Blood Bowl House with a fortune. Mr Nicholls in his notes on the print gives the name of Blood-Bowl to the Alley, but there is no evidence that it was ever officially known by this name. The alley is Hanging-Sword Alley in Rocque's map of 1746; it bears the same name in Hatton's *New View*, 1708, and in Stow's *Survey of London* we read: 'Then is Water Lane, running down by the west side of a house called the Hanging Sword, to the Thames.' The alley appears under this name in various books giving the names of streets: it was Hanging-Sword Alley when Dickens wrote *Bleak House* and it is Hanging-Sword Alley today, a tiny alley off of Fleet Street.

1749, February 20 Usher Gahagan was executed at Tyburn. Gahagan was a scholar. He edited Brindley's edition of the classics, and translated into Latin verse Pope's *Essay on Criticism*. He also, while in prison, translated into Latin verse Pope's *Temple of Fame* and *Messiah* 'with a Latin Dedication to his Grace the Duke of Newcastle'. His offence was filing gold money.

1749, October 18 Fifteen malefactors were executed at Tyburn. There had been a riot in the Strand, where a number of sailors had wrecked a house in which a sailor had been maltreated. There exists a well-known print of the riot. The *London Magazine* gives the following account of the execution: 'about nine in the morning the criminals were put into the carts. Mr Sheriff Janssen, holding his white wand, and on horseback, attended the execution, accompanied by his proper officers. At Holborn-bars Mr Sheriff dismissed very civilly the party of foot-guards, who otherwise would have marched to Tyburn. The multitude of spectators was infinite. Though a rescue had been threatened by many (on account of Wilson and Penlez, the two ill-fated young rioters, both of whom were expected to suffer) there yet was not the least disturbance, except during a moment at the gallows, where a vast body of sailors, some of whom were armed with cutlasses, and all with bludgeons, began to be very clamorous as the unhappy sufferers were going to be turned off, which Mr Sheriff perceiving, he rode up to them and enquired in the mildest terms the reason of their tumult. Being answered that they only wanted to save the bodies of their brethren from the surgeons, and the Sheriff promising that the latter should not have them, the sailors thanked the above magistrate, wished every blessing to attend him, and assured him that they had no design to interrupt him in the execution of his office. The criminals seemed very penitent, and were turned off about twelve.'

1750, August 8 Six executed at Tyburn. 'It is remarkable that the above six malefactors suffered for robbing their several prosecutors of no more than six shilling' (*London Magazine*).

1750, October 3 Twelve malefactors executed at Tyburn. One of them was the celebrated 'Gentleman Highwayman', Mr Maclean. Another was William Smith, the son of a clergyman in Ireland. Smith was convicted of forgery. Smith had in an advertisement 'entreated contributions for his decent interment, and that his poor body might not fall unto the surgeons, and perpetuate the disgrace of his family'. According to a newspaper of the time the surgeons got possession of one body only (not Smith's): the rest were delivered to the friends. Smith edited several volumes of 'classicks'. The publisher seized the opportunity to advertise them. The first Sunday after his condemnation three thousand people went to see him. He fainted away twice with the heat of his cell. He was only twenty-six when executed. A long account of his behaviour in prison was given in a pamphlet by the Rev. Dr Allen. The rev. gentleman was greatly concerned to know whether Maclean, by his association with 'licentious young People of Figure and Fortune' who affected to despise 'all the principles of Natural and Revealed Religion, under the polite Name of Free-thinking' had not 'fallen into the fashionable way of thinking and talking on these Subjects.' Maclean was able to give his reverend monitor satisfactory assurances on this point. Maclean's brother was the minister of the English church at The Hague. Maclean lived in fashionable lodgings in St James's Street, and frequented masquerades, where he at times won or lost considerable sums. The skeleton of Maclean appears in the fourth plate of Hogarth's *Stages of Cruelty*, showing the interior of Surgeons' Hall.

1751, February 9 Three boy-burglars executed at Tyburn.

1753, June 7 Dr Archibald Cameron, condemned for high treason for being concerned 'in the late rebellion' and not surrendering in time. It might have been expected that vengeance would have been satiated by the numerous executions that had already taken place: then, too, the 'late rebellion' was eight years old. Dr Cameron was nevertheless sentenced to be drawn, hanged, and quartered. The quartering was omitted. He was, moreover, suffered to hang for twenty minutes, so that the burning of his bowels was done before eyes closed in death. Dr Cameron met death, not so much with fortitude, which implies, in a way, an effort, as with perfect equanimity.

1758, December 18 Some surgeons attempting to carry off the body of a man executed at Tyburn, the mob opposed, a riot ensued, in which several persons were wounded. In the end the mob was victorious, and carried off the body in triumph.

1759, June 18–October 3 In this year the old triangular gallows, in use for nearly two hundred years, was removed, and the new 'movable' gallows took its place.

1760, May 5 Earl Ferrers had more than one relative of unsound mind: he himself had given many proofs of madness. Without any cause, he shot his steward, who had been for thirty years in his service. He was undoubtedly a homicidal lunatic who would today be confined in an asylum. On his trial by the House of Lords he produced witnesses to prove his insanity, but his 'Lordship managed this defence himself in such a manner as showed perfect recollection of mind, and an uncommon understanding'. The plea was not accepted, the earl was sentenced to death. Under the ferocious Act of 1752 the execution should have taken place the next day but one, but, in consideration of the earl's rank, the execution was deferred to 5 May. The sentence, however, bore that the body should be anatomised. On the appointed day the earl rejected the mourning coach provided by his friends, and obtained permission to make the journey from the Tower to Tyburn in his own landau, drawn by six horses. He was dressed in a suit of light-coloured clothes, embroidered with silver, said to be his wedding suit. To the sheriff he said: 'You may perhaps, sir, think it strange to see me in this dress, but I have my particular reasons for it.' The procession was the grandest that had ever made that fatal journey. First came a very large body of Middlesex constables, preceded by one of the high constables: then a party of horse grenadiers, and a party of foot soldiers. Mr Sheriff Errington in his chariot, accompanied by his under-sheriff. The landau, escorted by two other parties of soldiers. Mr Sheriff Vaillant's chariot, carrying the sheriff and under-sheriff. A mourning coach, and six with some of his Lordship's friends. A hearse and six, provided for the conveyance of his Lordship's corpse from Tyburn to Surgeons' Hall. The procession was two hours and three quarters on the way, which gave time to the chaplain to worry the earl about his religion the world would naturally be very inquisitive concerning the religion his Lordship professed. His Lordship replied that he did not think himself accountable to the world for his sentiments on religion. He greatly blamed my Lord Bolingbroke for permitting his sentiments on religion to be published to the world. But he did not believe in salvation by faith alone. He gave his watch to Sheriff Vaillant, and intended to give five guineas to the hangman. By mischance it was to the hangman's assistant that the earl handed the money, whence arose a dispute between these officers of the

State. The enjoined dissection was performed perfunctorily; the body was publicly exposed in a room for three days, and then given up to friends. There exists an engraving showing the body as exposed in the coffin. Walpole gives a long account of the execution. It was remarkable, among other things, for the introduction of a new device. 'Under the gallows was a new-invented stage, to be struck from under him ... As the machine was new, they were not ready at it: his toes touched it, and he suffered a little, having had time by their bungling to raise his cap: but the executioner pulled it down again, and they pulled his legs, so that he was soon out of pain, and quite dead in four minutes.' The 'drop' was no more used at Tyburn, but it became a feature of the new gallows of Newgate. Walpole says that 'the executioners fought for the rope, and the one that lost it cried'. There is a story that Ferrers was hanged by a silk rope, or, in another version, that he desired to be hanged by such a rope. Timbs, in his *Curiosities of London* even asserts that the bill for this rope of silk is still in existence; he does not say where. The legend must have arisen later. It is a detail which would have delighted Walpole; he mentions the rope, as we have seen; his silence as to its particular character seems conclusive.

1767 Mrs Brownrigg, the wife of James Brownrigg, at one time a domestic servant, was the mother of a large family. To support the household Mrs Brownrigg learnt midwifery, and received an appointment as midwife to women in the workhouse of St Dunstan's-in-the-West. She had the character of being skilful and humane: she was reputed to be a faithful wife and an affectionate mother. About 1763 Brownrigg took a house in Fetter Lane, and in February, 1765, Mrs Brownrigg took as apprentice a poor girl of the precinct of Whitefriars: a little later another girl was bound apprentice to her by the governors of the Foundling Hospital. Mrs Brownrigg treated these poor girls with unimaginable cruelty. She tied them up naked, and flogged them with a horse-whip, made her husband and son do the same: starved them and gave them insufficient clothing. This went on for two years. At last the neighbours, constantly hearing groans in the Brownriggs' house, watched, and at last caught sight of one of the poor creatures in a most deplorable condition. Information was given and the girls were rescued. But relief came too late to save Mary Clifford, who died of the most terrible wounds inflicted on her by these monsters. On 12 September, father, mother, and eldest son were tried for the murder of Mary Clifford: only Elizabeth Brownrigg was found guilty. She was executed on 14 September, her body was carried to Surgeons' Hall to be anatomised. Afterwards 'her skeleton has since been exposed in the niche opposite the first door in the Surgeons' Theatre, that the heinousness of her cruelty may make the more lasting impression on the minds of the spectators'. *The Gentleman's Magazine* adds to a full account of the story an engraving showing the 'Hole' under the stairs in which the poor wretches were confined, and the kitchen in which one of the girls is shown tied up to be flogged. The case made a profound impression on the public.

1768, March 23 James Gibson, attorney-at-law, convicted of forgery, and Benjamin Payne, footpad, were executed at Tyburn. For a long time, as has been shown, the 'respectability' of criminals had been recognised by permitting them to be carried to their doom in a mourning coach, instead of in the ordinary cart. To Gibson, as the erring member of an honoured profession, this indulgence was granted. Gibson desired that the footpad might be allowed to accompany him in the coach. There is something pathetic in this practical recognition of the truth that death makes all men equal. The authorities might well have granted the request, but it was refused.

1771 On October 16, Mary Jones was executed at Tyburn for stealing from a draper's shop on Ludgate Hill some pieces of worked muslin. The annals of Tyburn contain the record of no more poignant tragedy than this. It is a story so piteous that, once heard, it ever after haunts the memory. Mary Jones was a young woman whose age is variously given as nineteen and twenty-six: all accounts tell of her great beauty. She was married, lived in good credit, and wanted for nothing till her husband was carried off by a press-gang. Then she fell into great straits, having neither a bed to lie on, nor food to give to her two young children, who were almost naked. On her trial her defence was simple: 'I have been a very honest woman in my lifetime. I have two children: I work very hard to maintain my two children since my husband was pressed.' Her beauty and her poverty prove Mary's averment that she had been a very honest woman. But when the jury gave in a verdict of guilty, Mary cursed judge and jury for a lot of 'old fogrums'. It was really for this that she died on the gallows. The theft had not been completed: she was arrested in the shop and gave up the goods. It was her first offence. Her neighbours in Red Lion street, Whitechapel, presented a petition in her behalf, but there was against her the record of her 'indecent behaviour'. One of the two children was at her breast when she set out in the cart on the journey from Newgate to Tyburn. 'Her petulance had gone: she met death with amazing fortitude.' So perished Mary Jones, whose husband had been torn from her side, who was now, in her turn, torn from her helpless babes.

1773, September 13 Mrs Herring was executed for murdering her husband: she was placed on a stool something more than two feet high, and, a chain being placed under her arms, the rope round her neck was made fast to two spikes, which, being driven through a post against which she stood, when her devotions were ended, the stool was taken from under her, and she was soon strangled. When she had hung about fifteen minutes, the rope was burnt, and she sunk till the chain supported her, forcing her hands up to a level with her face, and the flame being furious, she was soon consumed. The crowd was so immensely great that it was a long time before the faggots could be placed for the execution.

1773, October 27 The two sheriffs and under-sheriff attended the execution of five malefactors on horseback, and two persons clothed in black walked all the way before the prisoners to the place of execution, where they were allowed an hour and a half in their devotions, a circumstance not remembered for a great many years past.

1776, January 17 Robert and Daniel Perreau executed at Tyburn. They were twin brothers, natives of St Kitts. Robert was an apothecary 'in high practice' in Golden Square, then a fashionable quarter. Daniel lived a genteel life 'with his mistress', Mrs Rudd. Robert Perreau sought a loan of Drummonds, the bankers, on bonds, afterwards found to be forged. The evidence made it probable that the actual forgery was by Mrs Rudd, but that all three were acting in concert. The brothers were both found guilty on their trials, but a strong feeling existed that the sentence on Robert was harsh. A petition to commute the sentence to one of transportation was presented on behalf of seventy-eight 'capital Bankers and Merchants' of the City. The king was, however, obdurate, and after the acquittal of Mrs Rudd let the law take its course. The execution was witnessed by 30,000 persons. The brothers, born together, were not divided in death. They fell from the cart with their four hands clasped together. Mr Bleackley has told the story at length in *Some Distinguished Victims of the Scaffold*, 1905.

1777, June 27 Execution of Dr Dodd. William Dodd, born in 1729, was the popular preacher of his day. He came, a young man of 21, from Cambridge to London in 1750. He hesitated between adopting literature as a profession and the Church, but took orders in 1751. He still dabbled in literature, and is said to have been the author of a work, *The Sisters*, which gave no very favourable idea of the purity of his mind. In 1758 he became chaplain of the Magdalen Hospital, and fine ladies came to hear his sermons 'in the French style'. In 1763 he was made one of the king's chaplains, an appointment he lost when, in 1774, Mrs Dodd wrote to the wife of the Lord Chancellor, offering a bribe for the living of St George, Hanover Square. Dodd got into debt: he had to sell a proprietary chapel in which he had sunk money: it is said that he even 'descended so low as to become the editor of a newspaper'. He fell still lower: in his need he forged the signature of his patron, Lord Chesterfield, to a bond for £4,200. The forgery was discovered, and warrants were issued against Dodd and his broker. Dodd made partial restitution, offered security for the remainder, and the affair might have been settled had not the Lord Mayor, who had issued the warrants, refused to let the case be hushed up. Dodd was tried on 22 February 1766. The evidence was irresistible. Only a legal point stood in the way of sentence. This point was decided adversely to Dodd, and on 26 May sentence of death was passed. 'They will never hang me,' said Dodd, and indeed everything possible was done to save him. 'The exertions made to save him were perhaps beyond example in any country. The newspapers were filled with letters and paragraphs in his favour. Individuals of all ranks and degrees exerted themselves in his behalf: parish officers went from house to house to procure subscriptions to a petition to the king, and this petition, which, with the names, filled twenty-three sheets of parchment, was actually presented. The Lord Mayor and Common Council went in a body to St James's, to solicit mercy for him, but all this availed nothing; government were resolved to make an example of him.'

Foremost among those who pleaded for Dodd was Dr Johnson. There was nothing in common between the shallow flippancy of Dodd, and the great, rough, earnest nature of Johnson; being once asked whether Dodd's sermons were not addressed to the passions, 'They were nothing, Sir,' growled the lexicographer, 'be they addressed to what they may.' But to misery Johnson's heart was more tender than a woman's; he was agitated when application was made to him on behalf of Dodd; he paced up and down the room, and promised to do what he could. He wrote the speech delivered by Dodd before the passing of the sentence and more than one petition in his behalf. All was in vain: 'If I pardon Dodd, I shall have murdered the Perreaus.' So the king is reported to have said and, indeed, although Dodd's partisans fell foul of court and jury, it is not easy to see how, if Dodd had been pardoned, the punishment of death for forgery could ever after have been inflicted. There is a pathetic touch in the fact that, many years before his fall, Dodd preached a sermon, afterwards printed, deprecating the frequency of capital punishment. In *Prison Thoughts* he foretold the abolition of the procession to Tyburn, or perhaps of public executions: 'yes, the day I joy in the idea will arrive When Britons philanthropic shall reject The cruel custom, to the sufferer cruel, Useless and baneful to the gaping crowd!' On 27 June the fatal procession set out from Newgate. On this occasion 'there was perhaps the greatest concourse of people ever drawn together by a like spectacle'. Just before the parties were turned off Dr Dodd whispered to the executioner. What he said cannot be known; but it was observed that the man had 'no sooner driven away the cart, than he ran immediately under the gibbet, and took hold of the doctor's legs, as if to steady the body.' Another account says that the executioner, gained over by Dodd's friends, had arranged the knot in a particular manner, and whispered to him as the cart drew off, 'You must not move an inch!' When cut down the body was conveyed to the house of an undertaker in Goodge Street, where a hot bath was in readiness. Under the direction of Pott, a celebrated surgeon of the day, every effort was made to restore animation. But in vain. The crowd was so enormous that there had been great delay in the transport of the body, and this was fatal. Nevertheless, there were not wanting people who believed that Dodd had been resuscitated and carried abroad.

1779, April 19 The Rev. James Hackman executed at Tyburn for the murder of Miss Martha Ray. 'As the spectators were leaving the performance of *Love in a Village* at Drury Lane, on the night of 7 April, a gentleman, seeing Miss Ray, with whom he had some little acquaintance, in difficulty in getting to her coach, stept forward and offered his assistance, When close to the coach he heard the report of a pistol, and felt the lady fall. For a moment he thought that she had fallen in fright at the report, but on stooping down, to help her to rise, he found his hands covered with blood. With the aid of a light-boy, he got the lady into the Shakespeare tavern. She was dead.' The murdered woman was Miss Martha Ray, the mistress of Lord Sandwich, First Lord of the Admiralty; her murderer the Rev. Mr Hackman. Hackman was born in 1752. He was apprenticed to a mercer, but, disliking the business, his friends bought for him a commission in a foot regiment. While with a recruiting party at Huntingdon, he was invited to the country house of Lord Sandwich, and fell violently in love with the Earl's mistress. In 1776 he left the army, took orders, and in 1779 was presented to the living of Wiverton, in Norfolk. It is doubtful whether he ever officiated there. He had not been able to forget Martha Ray. He continued his attentions, and offered her marriage. On the fatal day, having written a letter to a friend, announcing his intention to destroy himself, he went to the theatre armed with two pistols. After discharging one at the lady, he shot himself and fell at the lady's feet, beating his head with the butt-end of a pistol and calling on the bystanders to kill him. On his trial his only defence was that a momentary frenzy overcame him. The letter contained nothing to indicate an intention to kill Miss Ray. He was executed on 19 April.

1779, August 25 Four malefactors were carried to Tyburn for execution, and had been tied up for near twenty minutes when a report was spread that a reprieve was come to Newgate for one of them. They were all untied and left in the cart while one of the sheriffs went to Lord Weymouth to learn the truth. No reprieve having been granted, the execution took place at near one o'clock.

1779, October 27 Isabella Condon, condemned for coining, was at Tyburn first strangled, and then burnt.

1781, July 27 Francis Henry de la Motte, executed at Tyburn for giving to the French Government information as to the movement of British ships. The sentence was in the usual form for high treason, that he should be hanged 'but not till you are dead', but he was allowed to hang for nearly an hour. The head was severed from the body, four incisions made in the body, and part of the entrails thrown into a fire. Then the body was delivered to an undertaker, and was buried in St Pancras churchyard.

1783, November 7 On this day took place the last execution at Tyburn. The occasion requires us to give in full the account, not otherwise particularly interesting. It is quoted from *The Gentleman's Magazine*: 'This morning was executed at Tyburn, John Austin, convicted the preceding Saturday of robbing John Spicer, and cutting and wounding him in a cruel manner. From Newgate to Tyburn he behaved with great composure. While the halter was tying, his whole frame appeared to be violently convulsed. The Ordinary having retired, he addressed himself to the populace: "Good people, I request your prayers for the salvation of my departing soul: let my example teach you to shun the bad ways I have followed: keep good company, and mind the word of God." The cap being drawn over his face, he raised his hands and cried, "Lord have mercy on me: Jesus look down with pity on me: Christ have mercy on my poor soul!" and, while uttering these words, the cart was driven away. The noose of the halter having slipped to the back part of his neck, it was longer than usual before he was dead.'

4
The Burial of the Dead

Punishment did not end with death. It was not uncommon during the eighteenth century to have one's body after death passed on to the surgeons for dissection. Many thousands were buried in pits in the immediate vicinity of the gallows: and many were not even buried at all, having their corpses hanged inside a metal case (a gibbet) by the side of a main highway, or on one of London's Heaths until birds and nature had eaten the corpse away. The Great West Road – now the A4 – that ran into London in the vicinity of Hounslow and into Knightsbridge was lined with the decaying corpses of former highwaymen, as was Hounslow Heath. The Rocque maps of London dating from the mid-eighteenth century show the gibbets littered throughout London, and along the banks of the Thames. The latter was meant to be a warning to visiting seamen. Burial of the condemned had often been a contentious issue. The historian Stow tells how, in 1348, Ralph Stratford, Bishop of London, bought a piece of ground, called No Man's Land, which he enclosed with a wall of brick, and dedicated for burial of the dead: this was Pardon churchyard.

> He there erected a small chapel, where masses were said for the repose of the dead, and named the place Pardon Churchyard. The plague still raging Sir Walter de Manny, that brave knight whose deeds are so proudly and prominently blazoned in the pages of Froissart, purchased of the brethren of St Bartholomew Spital a piece of ground contiguous to Pardon Churchyard, called the Spital Croft, which the good Bishop Stratford also consecrated.[66]

Here, we are told, were buried more than 50,000 persons who died of the Black Death. In 1371 Sir Walter founded the Charterhouse, giving to the monastery the thirteen acres, and also the three acres adjoining, 'which remained till our time [1598] by the name of Pardon churchyard, [at Charterhouse] and served for burying of such as desperately ended their lives, or were executed for felonies, who were fetched thither usually in a close cart, bailed over and covered with black, having a plain white cross thwarting, and at the fore end a St John's cross without, and within a bell ringing by shaking of the cart, whereby the same might be heard when it passed: and this was called the friary cart, which belonged to St John's, and had the privilege of sanctuary.'[67] In the *Grey Friars' Chronicle* which covers the period from Richard I (1157–99) to Mary I (1516–58), we find an instance of the burial in Pardon churchyard of persons executed at Tyburn:

> 1537. Also this yere the 25 day of Marche the Lyncolnecheremen that was with bishoppe Makerelle was browte owte of Newgate unto the yelde-halle [Guildhall] in roppys, and there had their jugment to be drawne, hangyd, and heddyd, and qwarterd, and soo was the 29 of Marche after, the wyche was on Maundy Thursdaye, and alle their qwarteres with their heddes was burryd at Pardone churcheyerde in the frary.

Stow tells us that the victims were twelve Lincolnshire men. The Reformation saw the priory of St John's dissolved in 1540, and with it went the friary cart. Thereafter bodies were brought back by friends for interment in the parish churchyard. There are records of bodies being refused burial here: One man executed at Tyburn for 'sparcing abrood certen lewed, sedicious, and traytorous bookes was brought into St Pulchers [St Sepulchres, opposite the now Old Bailey] to be buryed, but the parishioners would not suffer a Traytor's corpes to be layed in the earthe where theire parents, wyeffs, chyldren, kynred, maisters, and old neighbors did rest: and so his carcase was retourned to the buryall grounde neere Tyborne, and there I leave yt'. Many of the hanged had no friends to bury them. The *Grey Friars' Chronicle* tells of two priests and sixteen felons executed at the same time, in 1610, being all thrown together into a pit, which backs up accounts of bones found in the neighbourhood of the gallows. These may be the 'forgotten burial places or the pits into which, after a busy day's work, a score of bodies would be tumbled'. The historian John Strype (1643–1737), in his edition of Stow's *Survey*, tells of the finding of four embalmed heads in Blackfriars, in clearing away rubbish after the Great Fire of 1666:

> They came to an old Wall in a Cellar, of great thickness, where appeared a kind of Cupboard. Which being opened, there were found in it four Pots or Cases of fine Pewter, thick, with Covers of the same, and Rings fastened on the top to take up or put down at pleasure. The Cases were flat before, and rounding behind. And in each of them were reposited four humane Heads [he means one in each case; the margin has Four Heads, unconsumed, reserved as it seems, by Art; with their Teeth and Hair, the Flesh of a tawny Colour, wrap'd up in black Silk, almost consumed. And a certain Substance, of a blackish Colour, crumbled into Dust, lying at the bottom of the Pots. 'One of these Pots, with the Head in it, I saw in October, 1703, being in the Custody of Mr Presbury, then Sope-maker in Smithfield. Which Pot had inscribed in the inside of the Cover, in a scrawling Character (which might be used in the times of Henry VIII) J. CORNELIUS. This Head was without any Neck, having short red Hair upon it, thick, and that would not be pulled off ; and yellow Hair upon the Temples ; a little bald on the top (perhaps a Tonsure) the forepart of the Nose sunk, the Mouth gaping, ten sound Teeth, others had been plucked out ; the skin like tanned Leather, the Features of the Face visible. There was one Body found near it buried, and without a Head; but no other Bodies found. The other three Heads had some of the Necks joined to them, and had a broader and plainer Razure: which shewed them Priests. These three Heads are now dispersed. One was given to an Apothecary; Another was intrusted with the Parish Clerk; who it is thought got Money by shewing of it. It is probable they were at last privately procured, and conveyed abroad; and now become Holy Relicks.

They were probably priests or friars executed for treason; the Roman Catholic Dr Richard Challoner (1691–1781) tells the story relating to one of these heads. John Cornelius, or Mohun, who studied at Oxford, but 'not adopting the new religion' went afterwards to Rheims, and later to Rome. We are told that:

> He was sent upon the English mission, in which he laboured for about ten years. He was apprehended in April, 1594, in the house of the widow of Sir John Arundel, on the information of a servant of the house. Mr Bosgrave, a kinsman of

Sir John Arundel, seeing him hurried away without a hat, put his own hat on the priest's head; for this he was arrested. Two servants of the family, Terence Carey and Patrick Salmon, were also arrested. Cornelius was sent to London, and there racked to make him give up the names of Catholics who had harboured him. Refusing to make any discovery, he was sent back into the country, tried, and, with his three companions, executed at Dorchester on July 2, 1594. The three were simply hanged: Cornelius, as guilty of high treason, was drawn, hanged, and quartered. His head was nailed to the gallows, but afterwards removed at the instance of the town. His quarters were buried together with the bodies of his companions. Dr Challoner does not tell how the head of Cornelius was recovered by friends, nor does he say anything more of the others. It is probable that the three other heads of Strype's account were those of the companions of Cornelius.[68]

The Times of 9 May 1860, contained a letter from Mr A. J. Beresford Hope, living in the house at the south-west corner of Edgware Road, Arklow House in Connaught Place, stating:

Sir, The site of the Tyburn gallows has been a frequent subject of discussion among London antiquaries. It may be interesting to those who care for such questions to learn that yesterday, in the course of some excavations connected with the repair of a pipe in the roadway, close to the foot pavement along the garden of this house, at the extreme south-west angle of the Edgware-road, the workmen came upon numerous human bones. These were obviously relics of the unhappy persons buried under the gallows.

It is certain that the remains of Oliver Cromwell, Henry Ireton, and John Bradshaw, all condemned posthumously for the death of Charles I, lie in this vicinity. Prior to the return of Charles II in 1660 all three regicides had been buried in Westminster Abbey. On 30 January 1661, the twelfth anniversary of the execution of Charles I outside Whitehall Palace, Cromwell's body was removed from its tomb in the Abbey, and was posthumously executed on the Tyburn gallows. The remains of Bradshaw and Ireton suffered the same fate. After the bodies had hung in chains they were thrown into a pit and Cromwell's head was placed on a pole outside Westminster Hall where it remained until 1685. Pepys, in his diary of Tuesday 4 December 1660, comments:

This day the Parliament voted the bodies of Oliver, Ireton, Bradshaw, &c., should
be taken up out of their graves in the Abbey, and drawn to the gallows, and there
hanged and buried under it: which (methinks) do trouble me that a man of so
great courage as he was, should have that dishonour, though otherwise he might
deserve it enough.

A stone slab in the RAF chapel of Westminter Abbey records 'these
[remains] were removed in 1661'. The Cromwell vault was then
used for the last resting place of the illegitimate descendants of
Charles II. Cromwell's head, after allegedly blowing down from its
spike in a storm, went on a series of travels before being buried in
the grounds of his old college, Sidney Sussex College, Cambridge,
in 1960.

Further evidence of burials in the vicinity of Marble Arch come
from an inhabitant of the area born about 1750 who stated that 'I
have every reason to believe that the space from the toll-house [on
the junction of the Edgware Road and Oxford Street] to Frederick
Mews was used as a place of execution, and the bodies buried
adjacent, for I have seen the remains disinterred when the square
and adjoining streets were being built'.[69]

Today there are a few reminders of what once stood in the
vicinity of Marble Arch.

5

Attending an Execution

There are many contemporary reports of what it was like to attend a London execution. These reports tend to reflect an evolution of thought that progresses in the sixteenth century from a matter-of-fact enjoyment of watching an execution, very much in the same vein as one might attend some sporting match today, to a more circumspect approach which can be seen in eighteenth century accounts and reaching a thoughtful questioning approach in the nineteenth century. The diarist James Boswell (1740–95) wrote:

> I must confess that I myself am never absent from a public execution … when I first attended them I was shocked to the greatest degree. I was in a manner convulsed with pity and terror, and for several days, but especially the night after, I was in a very dismal situation. Still, however I persisted in attending them and by degrees my sensibility abated; so that I can now see one with great composure … the curiosity which impels people to be present at such affecting scenes is certainly a proof of sensibility, not callousness. For it is observed that the greatest proportion of spectators is composed of women.

The writer Samuel Richardson (1689–1761) published a report in the form of a letter of what the Tyburn experience involved.

> Dear Brother, I have this day been satisfying a Curiosity I believed natural to most People, by seeing an Execution at Tyburn. The Sight has had an extra-ordinary Effect upon me, which is more owing to the unexpected Oddness of the scene, than the affecting Concern which is unavoidable in a thinking Person, at a Spectacle so awful, and so interesting, to all who consider themselves of the same Species with the unhappy Sufferer.

Richardson continues and describes how he joined the procession of the prisoner who was being kept at Newgate prior to his last journey through Holborn, and via St Giles, to the gallows:

> That I might the better view the Prisoners, and escape the Pressure of the Mob, which is prodigious, nay, almost incredible, if we consider the Frequency of these Executions in London, which is once a Month, I mounted my Horse, and accompanied the melancholy Cavalcade from Newgate to the fatal Tree. The Criminals were Five in Number. I was much disappointed at the Unconcern and Carelessness

After 1783 the spectacle of execution shifted to the outside of Newgate Prison. What follows are haunting accounts of executions that took place, written by literate and thinking individuals who were very uncomfortable with what they witnessed. The first is a description from 1827 by a person who 'was allowed behind the scenes' of an execution morning at Newgate:

> No further delay was allowed. The sheriffs moved on, the ordinary, the culprits, and the officers did the same; and that class of attendants to which I belonged followed. I shall not easily forget the circumstances of this brief, but melancholy progress. The faltering step – the deep-drawn sigh – the mingling exclamations of anguish and devotion which marked the advance of the victims – the deep tones of the reverend gentleman who now commenced reading a portion of the burial service, and the tolling of the prison bell, which, as we proceeded through some of the most dreary passages of the gaol, burst on the ear, rendered the whole spectacle impressive beyond description. Few steps sufficed to conduct us to the small room, or entrance-hall, into which the debtor's door opens, and from this we saw the ladder which the criminals were to ascend, and the scaffold on which they were to die. I was on the alert to detect any sudden emotion which this spectacle might cause, but could not perceive that it had the slightest effect. The minds of the sufferers had been so prepared, that a partial view of the machine to which they were being conducted, seemed to give no additional shock. No further pause was deemed necessary. The clock was striking eight, and the ordinary and the youth first brought to the press-room, immediately passed up the ladder. To the two culprits that remained, the gentleman whom I have already mentioned offered his services, and filled up with a prayer the little interval which elapsed, before the second was conducted to the platform.
>
> I heard from without the murmur of awe, of expectation, and pity, which ran

through the crowd in front of the prison, and stepping on a small erection to the left of the door, gained a momentary glimpse of a portion of the immense multitude, who, uncovered, and in breathless silence, gazed on the operations of the executioners. I retreated just as the third halter had been adjusted. The finisher of the law was in the act of descending, when the under-sheriff addressed him:

'Is everything quite ready?'

'Yes, sir.'

'Then take care and draw the bolt out smartly. Now, don't bungle it.'

'No, sir, you may depend upon it,' was the answer. And the obsequious anxiety of the hangman to seem polite and obliging, his apparent zeal to give satisfaction, though very natural seemed to me not a little curious.

Prayers, which had been interrupted for a moment, while the last awful ceremony was in progress, were resumed. As he read them, I saw the clergyman fix his eye on the executioner with a peculiar expression. He drew his handkerchief from his pocket, and passed it slightly over his upper lip. This was the fatal signal. A lumbering noise, occasioned by the falling of part of the apparatus, announced that it had been obeyed.

In that moment, a rush from the scaffold forced me from the door. The sheriffs, the under-sheriff, the ordinary, the gentleman who had assisted him in preparing the sufferers for eternity, and several other persons quitted the platform as expeditiously as possible, that they might not behold the final agonies of the unhappy men. Sir Thomas took me by the arm as he passed, and signified that he wished me to accompany him. I did so. Again I marched through the passages which I had recently traversed. Two minutes brought me to the door of the room to which I had first been conducted. Here my friend accosted me with his natural firmness of tone, which before had been considerably subdued by humane emotions, and said:

'You must breakfast with us.'

I started at the unsentimental idea of eating the moment after quitting so awful a spectacle, as that which I have attempted to describe. But I had not sufficient energy to resist the good will which rather unceremoniously handed me in. Here I found the other sheriff, the ordinary, the under-sheriff, the city-marshal, and one or two of the individuals I had previously met, already seated.

They partook of breakfast whilst the victims hanged for the required period of one hour. Breakfast was pleasant and a sense of ordinariness and even humour prevailed which whilst taking part in the merriment and quips, the writer displayed an uncomfortable awareness of the awfulness of the events which had just taken place. The visitor continues:

I and the rest of the company laughing heartily … The facetious sheriff now had it all his own way, and said several things ... We were thus pleasantly engaged, when the aide-de-camp of the gallant officer in the blue and gold – one of the city marshal's-men, entered to announce that it was past nine o'clock, and to ask if any of the company chose to see the bodies taken down.

'The bodies!' I repeated to myself, and the application of that word to those whom I had previously heard mentioned but by their names, recalled my thoughts which had somehow strayed from the business of the morning into unlooked-for cheerfulness, and presented, in that simple expression, an epitome of all that had moved my wonder, curiosity, and commiseration.

Again we passed through those parts of the prison which I had twice before traversed. We advanced with a quicker step than when following those whom we now expected to see brought to us. But with all the expedition we could use, on reaching the room from which the scaffold could be seen, we found the 'bodies' already there. Nor was this, in my opinion, the least striking scene which the morning brought under my observation. The dead men were extended side by side, on the stone floor. The few persons present gazed on them in silence, duly impressed with the melancholy spectacle. But in this part of the building a copper is established, in which a portion of the provisions for its inmates is prepared. There was a savoury smell of soup, which we could not help inhaling while we gazed on death. The cooks too were in attendance, and though they, as became them, did all in their power to look decorously dismal, well as they managed their faces, they could not so divest themselves of their professional peculiarities, as not to awaken thoughts which involuntarily turned to ludicrous or festive scenes. Their very costume was at variance with the general gloom, and no sympathy could at once repress the jolly rotundity of their persons.

An account by Captain Shaw, a witness to one of the last executions outside Newgate in 1864, describes his experience:

The scene on the night preceding a public execution afforded a study of the dark side of nature not to be obtained under any other circumstances. Here was to be seen the lowest scum of London densely packed together as far as the eye could see, and estimated by *The Times* at not less than 20,000. Across the entire front of Newgate heavy barricades of stout timber traversed the streets in every direction, erected as a precaution against the pressure of the crowd ... As the crowd increased wholesale highway robberies were of most frequent occurrence; and victims in the hands of some two or three desperate ruffians were as far from help as though divided by a continent from the battalions of police surrounding the scaffold.

Shaw paints a graphic picture of the scenes that unfolded on the evening prior to an execution when he opened the roller of his window through which he observed the execution:

The scene that met one's view on pulling up the windows ... and looking out on the black night sky and its blacker accompaniments baffles description. A surging mass, with here and there a flickering torch, rolled and roared before one; above this weird scene arose the voices of men and women shouting, singing, blaspheming, and, as the night advanced and the liquid gained firmer mastery, it seemed as if hell had delivered up its victims. To approach the window was a matter of danger; volleys of mud immediately saluted one, accompanied by more blaspheming and shouts of defiance. It was difficult to believe one was in the centre of a civilised capital that vaunted its religion and yet meted out justice in such a form.

Almost as if describing on-pitch activities prior to the commencement of a major football match, Shaw captures the dark atmosphere that existed outside what is now the Old Bailey in the early hours of the morning of execution. At 4 a.m. workmen appeared,

...immediately followed by a rumbling sound, and one realised that the scaffold was being dragged round. A grim, square, box-like apparatus was now distinctly visible, as it slowly backed against the debtors' door [the door through which the condemned appeared was one storey above the pavement]. Lights now flickered about the scaffold – the workmen fixing the cross-beams and uprights. Every stroke of the hammer must have vibrated through the condemned cells, and warned the wakeful occupants that their time was nearly come.

Much of the activity took place in and around the prison kitchen:

Meanwhile, a little unpretending door was gently opened; this was the 'debtor's door', and led directly through the kitchen on to the scaffold. The kitchen on these occasions was turned into a temporary mausoleum and draped with tawdry black hangings, which concealed the pots and pans, and produced an effect supposed to be more in keeping with the solemn occasion.

Shaw tells us that an 'old and decrepit man' made his appearance. This was the executioner, William Calcraft, who then proceeded to test the drop. By 7.30 a.m. the street theatre was almost due to begin:

The tolling of St Sepulchre's bell about 7.30 a.m. announced the approach of the hour of execution; meanwhile a steady rain was falling, though without diminishing the ever-increasing crowd. As far as the eye could reach was a sea of human faces. Roofs, windows, church-rails, and empty vans – all were pressed into service, and tightly packed with human beings. The rain had made the drop slippery, and necessitated precautions on behalf of the living if not of those appointed to die, so sand was thrown over a portion. The sand was for the benefit of the 'ordinary', the minister of religion, who was to offer the dying consolation at 8 a.m., and breakfast at 9.

The final act then commenced with the procession of the condemned winding its way through the kitchen. Shaw describes the condemned as a 'cadaverous mob, securely pinioned, and literally as white as marble'. He describes the sequence of events he observed on the platform:

As they reached the platform a halt was necessary as each was placed one by one immediately under the hanging chains. At the end of these chains were hooks which were eventually attached to the hemp round the neck of each wretch. The concluding ceremonies did not take long, considering how feeble the aged hangman was. A white cap was first placed over every face, then the ankles were strapped together, and finally the fatal noose was put around every neck, and the end attached to the hooks ... The silence was now awful. One felt one's heart literally in one's mouth, and found oneself involuntarily saying, 'They could be saved yet – yet – yet,' and then a thud that vibrated through the street announced that the felons were launched into eternity.

Shaw then reports on the seconds and minutes after the trap had opened:

One's eyes were glued to the spot and, fascinated by the awful sight, not a detail escaped one. Calcraft, meanwhile, apparently not satisfied with his handiwork, seized hold of one poor wretch's feet, and pressing on them for some seconds with all his weight, passed from one to another with hideous composure...

After the multitude had allowed the statutory hour to pass, during which the bodies remained suspended, Shaw informs us that the 'drunken again took up their ribald songs, conspicuous amongst which was one that had done duty pretty well through the night, and ended with "Calcraft, Calcraft, he's the man"'. The latter is reminiscent of a scene at a football match, following a well-executed goal. The show was now almost over with the exception of the removal of the bodies. When St Sepulchre chimed 9 o'clock, 'Calcraft, rubbing his lips, again appeared, and, producing a clasp knife, proceeded to hug the various bodies in rotation with one arm whilst with the other he severed the several ropes. It required two slashes of the feeble old arm to complete this final ceremony, and then the heads fell with a flop on the old man's breast...' Calcraft staggered under the weight and proceeded to 'jam' the bodies into their awaiting coffins. Shaw notes that then that the debtors' door 'closed till again required for a similar tragedy'.[70]

William Makepeace Thackeray (1811–63) and Charles Dickens (1812–70) attended executions and expressed their misgivings. Thackeray has left us a haunting, thoughtful and honest report of what it was like when he attended the execution of a Swiss valet, Courvoisier, who had murdered his employer Lord William Russell. The crowd was immense for the small area outside Newgate available: 40,000 people were present. Dickens and Thackeray both attended and were appalled by the experience. Both campaigned against capital punishment. It has been argued that the Courvoisier execution was a turning point in the capital punishment debate, although public executions would continue for another twenty-eight years until 1868. Thackeray has left us an account of the emotions involved in attending an execution:

X—, who had voted with Mr Ewart for the abolition of the punishment of death, was anxious to see the effect on the public mind of an execution, and asked me to accompany him to see Courvoisier killed. We had not the advantage of a sheriff's order, like the 'six hundred noblemen and gentlemen' who were admitted within the walls of the prison; but determined to mingle with the crowd at the foot of the scaffold, and take up our positions at a very early hour.

As I was to rise at three in the morning, I went to bed at ten, thinking that five hours' sleep would be amply sufficient to brace me against the fatigues of the coming day. But, as might have been expected, the event of the morrow was perpetually before my eyes through the night, and kept them wide open. I heard all the clocks in the neighbourhood chime the hours in succession; a dog from some court hard by kept up a pitiful howling; at one o'clock, a cock set up a feeble melancholy crowing; shortly after two the daylight came peeping grey through the window-shutters; and by the time that X— arrived, in fulfilment of his promise, I had been asleep about half-an-hour. He, more wise, had not gone to rest at all, but had remained up all night at the Club along with Dash and two or three more. Dash is one of the most eminent wits in London, and had kept the company merry all night with appropriate jokes about the coming event. It is curious that a murder is a great inspirer of jokes. We all like to laugh and have our fling about it; there is a certain grim pleasure in the circumstance – a perpetual jingling antithesis between life and death, that is sure of its effect.

In mansion or garret, on down or straw, surrounded by weeping friends and solemn oily doctors, or tossing unheeded upon scanty hospital beds, there were many people in this great city to whom that Sunday night was to be the last of any that they should pass on earth here. In the course of half-a-dozen dark wakeful hours, one had leisure to think of these (and a little, too, of that certain supreme night, that shall come at one time or other, when he who writes shall be stretched upon the last bed, prostrate in the last struggle, taking the last look of dear faces that have cheered us here, and lingering – one moment more – ere we part for the tremendous journey); but, chiefly, I could not help thinking, as each clock sounded, what is he doing now – has he heard it in his little room in Newgate yonder – Eleven o'clock. He has been writing until now, can hold out no longer, and is very weary. 'Wake me at four,' says he, 'for I have still much to put down.' From eleven to twelve the gaoler hears how he is grinding his teeth in his sleep. At twelve he is up in his bed and asks, 'Is it the time?' He has plenty more time yet for sleep; and he sleeps, and the bell goes on tolling. Seven hours more – five hours more. Many a carriage is clattering through the streets, bringing ladies away from evening parties; many bachelors are reeling home after a jolly night; Covent Garden is alive; and the light coming through the cell-window turns the gaoler's candle pale. Four hours more! 'Courvoisier,' says the gaoler, shaking him, 'it's four o'clock now, and I've woke you as you told me; but there's no call for you to get up yet.' The poor wretch leaves his bed, however, and makes his last toilet; and then falls to writing, to tell the world how he did the crime for which he has suffered. This time he will tell the truth and the whole truth. They bring him his breakfast 'from the coffee-shop opposite – tea, coffee, and thin bread and butter'. He will take nothing, however, but goes on writing. He has to write to his mother – the pious mother far away in his own country – who reared him and loved him; and even now has sent him her forgiveness and her blessing. He finishes his memorials and letters, and makes his will, disposing of his little miserable property of books and tracts that pious people have furnished him with. 'Ce 6 Juillet, 1840. Francois Benjamin Courvoisier vous donne ceci, mon ami, pour souvenir.' He has a token for his dear friend the gaoler; another for his dear friend the under-sheriff. As the day of the convict's death draws nigh, it is painful to see how he fastens upon everybody who approaches him, how pitifully he clings to them and loves them.

While these things are going on within the prison (with which we are made accurately acquainted by the copious chronicles of such events which are published subsequently), X—'s carriage has driven up to the door of my lodgings, and we have partaken of an elegant *dejeuner* that has been prepared for the occasion. A cup of coffee at half-past three in the morning is uncommonly pleasant; and X— enlivens us with the repetition of the jokes that Dash has just been making. Admirable, certainly – they must have had a merry night of it, that's clear; and we stoutly debate whether, when one has to get up so early in the morning, it is best to have an hour or two of sleep, or wait and go to bed afterwards at the end of the day's work. That fowl is extraordinarily tough — the wing, even, is as hard as a board; a slight disappointment, for there is nothing else for breakfast. 'Will any gentleman have some sherry and soda-water before he sets out? It clears the brains famously.' Thus primed, the party sets out. The coachman has dropped asleep on the box, and wakes up wildly as the hall-door opens. It is just four o'clock. About this very time they are waking up poor – pshaw! who is for a cigar? X— does not smoke himself; but vows and protests, in the kindest way in the world, that he does not care in the least for the new drab-silk linings in his carriage. Z—, who smokes, mounts, however, the box. 'Drive to Snow Hill,' says the owner of the chariot. The policemen who are the only people in the street, and are standing by, look knowing – they know what it means well enough.

How cool and clean the streets look, as the carriage startles the echoes that have been asleep in the corners all night. Somebody has been sweeping the pavements clean in the night-time surely; they would not soil a lady's white satin shoes, they are so dry and neat. There is not a cloud or a breath in the air, except X—'s cigar, which whiffs off, and soars straight upwards in volumes of white pure smoke. The trees in the squares look bright and green – as bright as leaves in the country in June. We who keep late hours don't know the beauty of London air and verdure; in the early morning they are delightful – the most fresh and lively companions possible. But they cannot bear the crowd and the bustle of mid-day. You don't know them then – they are no longer the same things. We have come to Gray's Inn; there is actually dew upon the grass in the gardens; and the windows of the stout old red houses are all in a flame.

As we enter Holborn the town grows more animated; and there are already twice as many people in the streets as you see at mid-day in a German *Residenz* or an English provincial town. The ginshop keepers have many of them taken their shutters down, and many persons are issuing from them pipe in hand. Down they go along the broad bright street, their blue shadows marching after them; for they are all bound the same way, and are bent like us upon seeing the hanging.

It is twenty minutes past four as we pass St Sepulchre's: by this time many hundred people are in the street, and many more are coming up Snow Hill. Before us lies Newgate Prison; but something a great deal more awful to look at, which seizes the eye at once, and makes the heart beat … There it stands black and ready, jutting out from a little door in the prison. As you see it, you feel a kind of dumb electric shock, which causes one to start a little, and give a sort of gasp for breath. The shock is over in a second; and presently you examine the object before you with a certain feeling of complacent curiosity. At least, such was the effect that the gallows produced upon the writer, who is trying to set down all his feelings as they occurred, and not to exaggerate them at all.

After the gallows-shock had subsided, we went down into the crowd, which was very numerous, but not dense as yet. It was evident that the day's business had not begun. People sauntered up, and formed groups, and talked; the new-comers asking those who seemed habitués of the place about former executions; and did the victim hang with his face towards the clock or towards Ludgate Hill? and had he the rope round his neck when he came on the scaffold, or was it put on by Jack Ketch afterwards – and had Lord W— taken a window, and which was he – I may mention the noble Marquis's name, as he was not at the exhibition.

Throughout the whole four hours, however, the mob was extraordinarily gentle and good-humoured. At first we had leisure to talk to the people about us…

A great number of coarse phrases are used, that would make ladies in drawing-rooms blush; but the morals of the men are good and hearty. A ragamuffin in the crowd (a powdery baker in a white sheep's-wool cap) uses some indecent expression to a woman near: there is an instant cry of shame, which silences the man, and a dozen people are ready to give the woman protection. The crowd has grown very dense by this time, it is about six o'clock, and there is great heaving, and pushing, and swaying to and fro; but round the women the men have formed a circle, and keep them as much as possible out of the rush and trample. In one of the houses, near us, a gallery has been formed on the roof. Seats were here let, and a number of persons of various degrees were occupying them. Several tipsy dissolute-looking young men, of the Dick Swiveller cast, were in this gallery. One was lolling over the sunshiny tiles, with a fierce sodden face, out of which came a pipe, and which was shaded by long matted hair, and a hat cocked very much on one side. This gentleman was one of a party which had evidently not been to bed on Sunday night, but had passed it in some of those delectable night-houses in the neighbourhood of Covent Garden. The debauch was not over yet, and the women of the party were giggling, drinking, and romping, as is the wont of these delicate creatures; sprawling here and there, and falling upon the knees of one or other of the males. Their scarves were off their shoulders, and you saw the sun shining down upon the bare white flesh, and the shoulder-points glittering like burning-glasses. The people about us were very indignant at some of the proceedings of this debauched crew, and at last raised up such a yell as frightened them into shame, and they were more orderly for the remainder of the day. The windows of the shops opposite began to fill apace, and our before-mentioned friend with ragged elbows pointed out a celebrated fashionable character who occupied one of them; and, to our surprise, knew as much about him as the *Court Journal* or the *Morning Post*. Presently he entertained us with a long and pretty accurate account of the history of Lady —, and indulged in a judicious criticism upon her last work. I have met with many a country gentleman who had not read half as many books as this honest fellow, this shrewd proletaire in a black shirt. The people about him took up and carried on the conversation very knowingly, and were very little behind him in point of information. It was just as good a company as one meets on common occasions. I was in a genteel crowd in one of the galleries at the Queen's coronation; indeed, in point of intelligence, the democrats were quite equal to the aristocrats. How many more such groups were there in this immense multitude of nearly forty thousand, as some say – How many more such throughout the country? I never yet, as I said before, have been in an English mob without the same feeling for the persons who composed it, and without wonder at the vigorous orderly good sense and intelligence of the people.

Really the time passed away with extraordinary quickness. A thousand things of the sort related here came to amuse us. First the workmen knocking and hammering at the scaffold, mysterious clattering of blows was heard within it, and a ladder painted black was carried round, and into the interior of the edifice by a small side door. We all looked at this little ladder and at each other – things began to be very interesting. Soon came a squad of policemen; stalwart rosy-looking men, saying much for City feeding; well-dressed, well-limbed, and of admirable good-humour. They paced about the open space between the prison and the barriers which kept in the crowd from the scaffold. The front line, as far as I could see, was chiefly occupied by blackguards and boys – professional persons, no doubt, who saluted the policemen on their appearance with a volley of jokes and ribaldry. As far as I could judge from faces, there were more blackguards of sixteen and seventeen than of any maturer age; stunted, sallow, ill-grown lads, in ragged fustian, scowling about. There were a considerable number of girls, too, of the same age: one that Cruikshank and Boz might have taken as a study for Nancy. The girl was a young thief's mistress evidently; if attacked, ready to reply without a particle of modesty; could give as good ribaldry as she got; made no secret (and there were several inquiries) as to her profession and means of livelihood.

But yonder, glittering through the crowd in Newgate Streets – the Sheriff's carriages are slowly making their way. We have been here three hours! Is it possible that they can have passed so soon? Close to the barriers where we are, the mob has become so dense that it is with difficulty a man can keep his feet. Each man, however, is very careful in protecting the women, and all are full of jokes and good-humour. The windows of the shops opposite are now pretty nearly filled by the persons who hired them. Many young dandies are there with moustaches and cigars; some quiet fat family-parties, of simple honest tradesmen and their wives, as we fancy, who are looking on with the greatest imaginable calmness, and sipping their tea. Yonder is the sham Lord W—, who is flinging various articles among the crowd; one of his companions, a tall, burly man, with large moustaches, has provided himself with a squirt, and is aspersing the mob with brandy-and-water. Honest gentleman! high-bred aristocrat! genuine lover of humour and wit! I would walk some miles to see thee on the treadmill, thee and thy Mohawk crew!

We tried to get up a hiss against these ruffians, but only had a trifling success; the crowd did not seem to think their offence very heinous; and our friend, the philosopher in the ragged elbows, who had remained near us all the time, was not inspired with any such savage disgust at the proceedings of certain notorious young gentlemen, as I must confess fills my own particular bosom. He only said, 'So-and-so is a lord, and they'll let him off,' and then discoursed about Lord Ferrers being hanged. The philosopher knew the history pretty well, and so did most of the little knot of persons about him, and it must be a gratifying thing for young gentlemen to find that their actions are made the subject of this kind of conversation.

Scarcely a word had been said about Courvoisier all this time. We were all, as far as I could judge, in just such a frame of mind as men are in when they are squeezing at the pit-door of a play, or pushing for a review or a Lord Mayor's show. We asked most of the men who were near us, whether they had seen many executions – most of them had, the philosopher especially; whether the sight of them did any good – 'For the matter of that, no; people did not care about them at all; nobody ever thought of it after a bit.' A countryman, who had left his drove in Smithfield, said the same thing; he had seen a man hanged at York, and spoke of the ceremony with perfect good sense, and in a quiet sagacious way...

It was past seven now; the quarters rang and passed away; the crowd began to grow very eager and more quiet, and we turned back every now and then and looked at St Sepulchre's clock. Half-an-hour, twenty-five minutes. What is he doing now? He has his irons off by this time. A quarter: he's in the press-room now, no doubt. Now at last we had come to think about the man we were going to see hanged. How slowly the clock crept over the last quarter! Those who were able to turn round and see (for the crowd was now extraordinarily dense) chronicled the time, eight minutes, five minutes; at last – ding, dong, dong, dong! – the bell is tolling the chimes of eight.

Between the writing of this line and the last, the pen has been put down, as the reader may suppose, and the person who is addressing him has gone through a pause of no very pleasant thoughts and recollections. The whole of the sickening, ghastly, wicked scene passes before the eyes again; and, indeed, it is an awful one to see, and very hard and painful to describe.

As the clock began to strike, an immense sway and movement swept over the whole of that vast dense crowd. They were all uncovered directly, and a great murmur arose, more awful, bizarre, and indescribable than any sound I had ever before heard. Women and children began to shriek horribly.

I don't know whether it was the bell I heard; but a dreadful quick feverish kind of jangling noise mingled with the noise of the people, and lasted for about two minutes. The scaffold stood before us, tenantless and black; the black chain was hanging down ready from the beam. Nobody came. 'He has been respited,' some one said; another said, 'He has killed himself in prison.'

Just then, from under the black prison-door, a pale quiet head peered out. It was shockingly bright and distinct; it rose up directly, and a man in black appeared on the scaffold, and was silently followed by about four more dark figures. The first was a tall grave man: we all knew who the second man was. 'That's he – that's he!' you heard the people say, as the devoted man came up.

I have seen a cast of the head since, but, indeed, should never have known it. Courvoisier bore his punishment like a man, and walked very firmly. He was dressed in a new black suit, as it seemed: his shirt was open. His arms were tied in front of him. He opened his hands in a helpless kind of way, and clasped them once or twice together. He turned his head here and there, and looked about him for an instant with a wild imploring look. His mouth was contracted into a sort of pitiful smile. He went and placed himself at once under the beam, with his face towards St Sepulchre's. The tall grave man in black twisted him round swiftly in the other direction, and, drawing from his pocket a night-cap, pulled it tight over the patient's head and face. I am not ashamed to say that I could look no more, but shut my eyes as the last dreadful act was going on which sent this wretched guilty soul into the presence of God.

If a public execution is beneficial – and beneficial it is, no doubt, or else the wise laws would not encourage forty thousand people to witness it – the next useful thing must be a full description of such a ceremony, and all its entourages, and to this end the above pages are offered to the reader. How does an individual man feel under it – in what way does he observe it – how does he view all the phenomena connected with it – what induces him, in the first instance, to go and see it – and how is he moved by it afterwards? The writer has discarded the magazine 'We' altogether, and spoken face to face with the reader, recording every one of the impressions felt by him as honestly as he could.

I must confess, then (for 'I' is the shortest word, and the best in this case), that the sight has left on my mind an extraordinary feeling of terror and shame. It seems to me that I have been abetting an act of frightful wickedness and violence, performed by a set of men against one of their fellows; and I pray God that it may soon be out of the power of any man in England to witness such a hideous and degrading sight. Forty thousand persons (say the Sheriffs), of all ranks and degrees – mechanics, gentlemen, pickpockets, members of both Houses of Parliament, street-walkers, newspaper-writers, gather together before Newgate at a very early hour; the most part of them give up their natural quiet night's rest, in order to partake of this hideous debauchery, which is more exciting than sleep, or than wine, or the last new ballet, or any other amusement they can have. Pickpocket and Peer each is tickled by the sight alike, and has that hidden lust after blood which influences our race. Government, a Christian Government, gives us a feast every now and then: it agrees – that is to say, a majority in the two Houses agrees – that for certain crimes it is necessary that a man should be hanged by the neck. Government commits the criminal's soul to the mercy of God, stating that here on earth he is to look for no mercy; keeps him for a fortnight to prepare, provides him with a clergymen to settle his religious matters (if there be time enough, but Government can't wait); and on a Monday morning, the bell tolling, the clergyman reading out the word of God, 'I am the resurrection and the life', 'The Lord giveth and the Lord taketh away', – on a Monday morning, at eight o'clock, this man is placed under a beam, with a rope connecting it and him; a plank disappears from under him, and those who have paid for good places may see the hands of the Government agent, Jack Ketch, coming up from his black hole, and seizing the prisoner's legs, and pulling them, until he is quite dead – strangled.

Many persons, and well-informed newspapers, say that it is mawkish sentiment to talk in this way, morbid humanity, cheap philanthropy, that any man can get up and preach about. There is the *Observer*, for instance, a paper conspicuous for the tremendous sarcasm which distinguishes its articles, and which falls cruelly foul of the *Morning Herald*. 'Courvoisier is dead,' says the *Observer*: 'he died as he had lived – a villain; a lie was in his mouth. Peace be to his ashes. We war not with the dead.' What a magnanimous Observer...

Look at the documents which came from the prison of this unhappy Courvoisier during the few days which passed between his trial and execution. Were ever letters more painful to read – at first, his statements are false, contradictory, lying. He has not repented then. His last declaration seems to be honest, as far as the relation of the crime goes. But read the rest of his statement, the account of his personal history, and the crimes which he committed in his young days, – then 'how the evil thought came to him to put his hand to the work', – it is evidently the writing of a mad, distracted man. The horrid gallows is perpetually before him; he is wild with dread and remorse. Clergymen are with him ceaselessly; religious tracts are forced into his hands; night and day they ply him with the heinousness of his crime, and exhortations to repentance. Read through that last paper of his; by Heaven, it is pitiful to read it.

There is some talk, too, of the terror which the sight of this spectacle inspires, and of this we have endeavoured to give as good a notion as we can in the above pages. I fully confess that I came away down Snow Hill that morning with a disgust for murder, but it was for the murder I saw done. As we made our way through the immense crowd, we came upon two little girls of eleven and twelve years: one of them was crying bitterly, and begged, for Heaven's sake, that some one would lead her from that horrid place. This was done, and the children were carried into a place of safety. We asked the elder girl – and a very pretty one – what brought her into such a neighbourhood? The child grinned knowingly, and said, 'We've koom to see the mon hanged!' Tender law, that brings out babes upon such errands, and provides them with such gratifying moral spectacles!

This is the 20th of July, and I may be permitted for my part to declare that, for the last fourteen days, so salutary has the impression of the butchery been upon me, I have had the man's face continually before my eyes; that I can see Mr Ketch at this moment, with an easy air, taking the rope from his pocket; that I feel myself ashamed and degraded at the brutal curiosity which took me to that brutal sight; and that I pray to Almighty God to cause this disgraceful sin to pass from among us, and to cleanse our land of blood.

6
Other London Places of Execution

Tyburn was probably the main and best-known place of execution in London until its demise in 1783. It was also, however, only one of many places where over the centuries criminals and political dissidents were executed. It was, as has been mentioned, extremely common for criminals to be executed at the scene of the crime. This meant that, as one unfortunate London inhabitant commented, it was 'possible to wake up on a morning and find a set of gallows being erected outside one's door.' Some of these random locations will be looked at, but the key locations were St Giles-in-the-Fields, behind Centre Point in Tottenham Court Road; Newgate, on the site of the present Old Bailey; Charing Cross, at the point in Trafalgar Square where the statue of Charles I on horseback stands; Old and New Palace Yards, by the Houses of Parliament; Tower Green; Tower Hill; St Paul's churchyard; Smithfield; Wapping, and Kennington Common. Other sites included Horsemonger Lane Gaol in Southwark, and Cheapside, opposite Bow church. These are but a few. The story of the random placing of execution is best told through a number of uprisings, and the sources of the time.

Peasant's Revolt, 1381
There were eighteen executions in London in one evening. The best-known victim was a 'quest-monger' (lawyer) named Roger Legett. Legett stood for everything that the rebels loathed: 'for years he had profited from dispensing partial justice and conniving with colleagues like the under-sheriff of London John Butterwick to obstruct, delay or deny due process of law and, therefore, the true and dutiful governance of England. He showed little concern for the

life or limb of those who crossed him.' Legett, aware that he was being hunted, fled to St Martin le Grand, no longer standing, which was famous for offering sanctuary.

The rebels burst into the chapel and dragged Legett down West Cheap to Cheapside, where 'at the confluence of Milk Street, Wood Street and Bread Street, they stopped. This was a well-known place of trade, conversation, preaching, water-gathering and public punishment. Legett was pushed to the ground.' He was beheaded in front of the Eleanor Cross.

Henry Machyn, a London clothier (1496/98–1563) kept a diary in which he recorded much relating to the insurrections and executions of his day. In his diary entry of 12 April 1554 he reveals a number of sites where executions took place after the Thomas Wyatt insurrection against Mary I, or Bloody Mary. Machyn tells us that Wyatt's head was 'set upon the gallows on Hay-Hill beside Hyde Park; where did hang 3 men in chains upon a stake'.[71]

Machyn wrote:

> The 8 day of February was commanded by the queen and the bishop of London that [St] Pauls and every Parish that they should sing *Te Deum Laudamus*, and ringing for the good victory that the queen['s] grace had against Wyatt and the rebellious of Kent, the which were over-come, thanks be unto God, with little blood-shed, and the residue taken and had to prison, and after were divers of them put to death in divers places in London and Kent.

Bloody Revenge

Queen Mary's revenge was swift. Many of the key parts of the City and many points outside such as Hyde Park Corner, the Strand, Fleet Street, Hay Hill, and Holborn had gallows erected in order that the consequences of the uprising could be observed by ordinary Londoners. Those who defected to Wyatt in the beginning, the 'White Coats', paid a heavy price. The chronicler Raphael Holinshed (1529–80) tells us that:

> … poore capytifs were brought forth, being so many in number, that all the prisons in London sufficed not to receive them, so that for lacke of place, they were faine to bestowe them in diverse Churches of the sayde Citie: and shortly after were set

up in London for a terrour to the common sort, (bycause the white coates beeing sent out of the Citie (as before ye have heard) revolted from the Queenes parte, to the aide of Wyat) twentie payre of Gallowes, on the which were hanged in severall places to the number of fiftie persons, which Gallowes remayned standing there a great part of the Sommer following, to the greate griefe of good Citizens, and for example to the Commitioners.

Machyn is more specific as to the locations of the gallows set up in London:

The 12 day of February was made at every gate in London a new pair of gallows and set up, 2 pair in Cheapside, 2 pair in Fleet Street, one in Smithfield, one pair in Holborn, one at Leaden-hall, one at saint Magnus London [Bridge], one at Pepper Alley gate, one at saint Georges [Southwark], one in Barunsaystret, one on Tower hill, one pair at Charing Cross, one pair beside Hyde park corner.

The 14 day of February were hanged at every gate and place: in Cheapside 6; Aldgate 1, quartered; at Leadenhall 3; at Bishopsgate one, and quartered Moorgate one; Cripplegate one; Aldersgate one, quartered Newgate one, quartered Ludgate one; Billingsgate 3 hanged; Saint Magnus 3 hanged; Tower hill 2 hanged; Holborn 3 hanged; Fleet Street 3 hanged; at Pepper alley gate 3; Barunsaystret 3; Saint Georges 3; Charing cross 4 ... at Hyde park corner 3, on Polard a waterbearer; theyre 3 hangs in chains; and but 7 quartered, and their bodies and heads set upon the gates of London.

The 16 day of February was made a great scaffold in Westminster hall for the duke of Suffolk.

The 17 day of February was the duke of Suffolk arraigned at Westminster hall, and cast for the treason, and cast to suffer death.

Henry Grey, Duke of Suffolk, was the father of Lady Jane Grey. The uprising had convinced Mary that it was now too dangerous to allow Lady Jane Grey and her husband Gilbert Dudley to remain alive in the Tower. Therefore on 12 February 1554 both she and her husband were executed. Five days after Jane's execution, Suffolk was brought to trial and found guilty of treason for his part in Dudley's scheme. He was beheaded on Tower Hill on 23 February 1554. The *Chronicle of the Grey Friars of London* reports:

Item the 12. of Februarij was beheddyd wythin the tower lady Jane that woulde a beene qweene; and hare husband whose name was Gylford Dudley at the Tower-hyll.

Item the 14 day of the same monyth for the same rebellyon was hangyd one Vicars, a yeoman of the guarde, Bouthe one of the queenes footmen, gret John Nortone, and one Kynge; and in severalle places abowte London at the gattes, in Chappe syde, (Cheapside) and other streettes, to the number of xxti, the wych ware of London that fled from the duke of Norfoke; and that same day was iij. hangyd in chanys on Hay hylle for the offence in rebellyon..

Wyatt was imprisoned in the White Tower, where he remained while he was tortured and attempts were made by the authorities to implicate Mary's half-sister Elizabeth in the plot. He witnessed the execution of Lady Jane Grey just six days before his own execution on 11 April.

The contemporary *Chronicle of Queen Jane* describes Wyatt's final day:

What was spoken is not yet knowen. Then he was brought out with a boke The xith of Aprell, being wenysdaye, was sir Thomas Wyat beheded upon Tower-hill. Before his coming downe out of the Tower, the lorde chamberlayne and the lorde shandos caryed him to the tower over the Watergaste, wher the lorde Courtney laye, and ther he was before Courtney half in his hande; and at the garden pale the lord chamberlayne tooke his leave of him, and likewise master secretarye Bourne, to whom master Wyat said: 'I praie you, sir, pray for me, and be a meane to the queen for my poor wife anmd children; and yf yt might have pleased her grace to have granted me my lyfe I would have trusted to have don hir such good service as shold have well recompenced myne offence; but since not, I beseche God have mercy on me.' To which master Bourne made no answer. So he came toward the [Tower] hill, Weston leading him by one arme and the lord Shandose by the other. Whe he was uppe apon the scaffold he desired eche man to praye for him and with him and said these or moche-like words in effecte: 'Good people, I am come presently here to dye, being thereunto lawfully and wourthely condemned, for I have sorely offended against God and the quenes majestie, and I am sorry therefore. I trust God hath forgiven and taken his mercy upon me. I besyche the queens majesty also of forgevenes.' 'She hath forgiven you allredy,' saith Weston. 'And let every man beware howe he taketh eny thinge in hande against the higher powers ... And I pray God I may be the last example in this place for that or eny other like. And whereas yt is said and wysled abroad, that I should accuse my lady

Elizabeth's grace, and my lorde Courtney; yt is not so, goode people, for I assure you neyther they nor eny other now.' And whether Mr Wyat, being the amased at such interruption, or whether they on the scaffold pluct him by the gown bake or no, yt is not well knowen, but without more talk he tourned him, and put of his gown and untrussyd his pointes, then, taking the [Earl of] Huntingdon, the lorde Hastinges, sir Giles Stranguesh, and many other by the hands, he plucked of his doblet and wastcote, unto his shirte, and knelyd downe upon the strawe, then laied his hed downe awhile, and rayse on his knees again , then after a few wourdes spoken, and his eyes lyft upp to heaven, he knytt the handekersheve himself about his eyes, ad a lyttel holding upp his hands suddenly laid downe his hed, which the hangeman at one stroke toke from him. Then was he forthwith quarteryd apon the scaffold, and the next day his quarters set at diverse places, and his hed apon a stake apon the gallos beyond saynte James. Which his hed, as ys reported, remained not there x.dayes unstolne awaye.

Wyatt was thirty-three years old when he died. His quartered body was then displayed in Newington, Mile End Green, St George's church, Southwark and beside St Thomas of Waterings. His head was placed on a pole at Hay Hill. On 17 April his head was stolen and never recovered.

The Protestant John Foxe published a book, *Acts and Monuments* (known usually as *The Book of Martyrs)*, in English in 1563, covering the sufferings of English Protestants from the fourteenth century through the reign of Mary I. Foxe tells us, in relation to Wyatt, that on 13 February 1554, 'were set up a great number of gallowses in divers places of the city; namely, two in Cheapside, one at Leadenhall, one at Billingsgate, one at St Magnus Church [by London Bridge], one in Smithfield, one in Fleet Street, four in Southwark, one at Aldgate, one at Bishopsgate, one at St James's Park corner, one at Cripplegate: and which gibbets and gallowses, to the number of twenty, there remained for terror of others from the thirteenth of February till the fourth of June and then, at the coming in of King Philip [of Spain], were taken down'.[72] Machyn tells us that on 8 April 1554 at the Cheapside gallows, a cat was hanged 'apparelled like a priest ready to say mass, with a shaven crown. Her two fore-feet were tied over her head, with a round paper-like wafer-cake put between them whereupon arose great evil-will against the City of London: for the queen [Mary I] and the bishops were very angry withal. And therefore the same afternoon there was a proclamation, that whosoever could bring forth the party that did hang up the cat, should have twenty nobles, which reward was after increased to twenty-marks; but none could or would earn it.'[73] We are told that towards the end of the reign of Elizabeth I, in the 1590s, a gallows was set up at the end of Tottenham Court Road in St Giles parish and that 'for two centuries the Holborn end of Fetter Lane, within a short distance of Red Lion Square, was no less frequently'. The *Newgate Calendar* of 1663 tells us that Colonel James Turner, charged with three robberies, upon being convicted:

> the usual sentence of death was passed on him, and he was executed on 21st of January, 1663, when he was drawn in a cart from Newgate to the end of Lime Street in Leadenhall Street, and there hanged on a gibbet erected for that purpose, being fifty-three years old.

The Gordon Riots of 1780 saw London again littered with temporary gallows. Some of the locations where the rioters were punished are easy to locate; some are quite vague. The cause of the anti-Catholic riots, Lord George Gordon, was tried before the Court of King's Bench, found not guilty of treason, and acquitted. Many of the rioters were not so fortunate. The *Newgate Chronicle* gives us the following information:

> Among those tried and convicted, were several women and boys; but not one individual of the smallest respectability or good fame; negroes, Jews, gypsies, and vagabonds of every description; the very refuse of society.
>
> Richard Roberts and William Lawrence, mere lads in appearance, hardly seventeen years of age, were among the principal leaders in these dreadful scenes of destruction, and were the first who were brought to trial. They were convicted of pulling down the house of Sir John Fielding, and hanged in Bow Street.
>
> Thomas Taplin, a captain-rioter, convicted of extorting money from Mr Mahon. That gentleman deposed that a ragged little boy came first up to him, and said, 'God bless your honour, some money for your poor mob!' He bid him begone. 'Then,' replied the imp of mischief, 'I'll call my captain.' Then came up the prisoner, Taplin, on horse-back, led by two boys, and attended by forty or fifty followers. Mr Mahon was intimidated, so as to purchase his security with half-a-crown. Taplin was also hanged in Bow Street, where he had stopped Mr Mahon.

George Kennedy, hanged in Bunhill-row, for pulling down the house of Mr M'Cartney, a baker.

William M'Donald, a cripple, who had lost an arm, and had formerly been a soldier, hanged on Tower-hill for destroying the house of J. Lebarty, a publican, in St Catharine's lane, near thereto.

James Henry, for setting fire to the house of Mr Langdon, on Holborn-hill.

George Bawton, a poor drunken cobbler, who meeting Mr Richard Stone, in High Street, Holborn, stopped him, saying, 'Pray remember the Protestant religion.' Mr Stone offered twopence, but the cobbler damned him, and swore he would have sixpence, which was complied with, for this he was hanged! a punishment which at any other time would have borne no proportion to the crime, and an instance of severity which we trust could not at any other time have occurred in England.

William Browne, for extorting money from Mr Daking, in Bishopsgate Street, as for the Protestant cause, and threatening to rip him up, if he did not comply.

William Bateman, executed in Coleman Street, for pulling down the house of Mr Charlton.

John Gray, Charles Kent, and Letitia Holland, hanged in Bloomsbury-square, for being a party to setting fire to the mansion of Lord Chief Justice Mansfield.

Mary Roberts and Charlotte Gardener, the latter a negress, hanged on Tower-hill for assisting to demolish the house of J. Lebarty, as before-mentioned.

Enoch Fleming, executed in Oxford-road, for assisting in pulling down the house of Ferdinand Schomberg.

George Staples, for being concerned in the riot in Moorfields, and assisting to pull down the Roman Catholic chapel there, and the house of James Malo.

Samuel Solomon, a Jew hanged in Whitechapel, for joining in the demolishing the house of Christopher Conner.

James Jackson, at the Old Bailey, convicted of setting fire to Newgate.

George Staples and Jonathan Stacy, also hanged in Moorfields, for being concerned in the riot, and burning of houses there.

Joseph Lovell and Robert Lovell, father and son, a pair of gypsies, hanged for aiding in setting fire to the house of Thomas Conolly.

The following, convicted of setting fire to the King's Bench Prison, and houses near thereto, were executed in St George's Fields, viz. Robert Loveli, Mary Cook, Edward Dorman, Elizabeth Collins, Henry Penny, and John Bridport.

Among the rioters, to sum up the account of their infamy and wretchedness, was Jack Ketch himself. This miscreant, whose real name was Edward Dennis, was convicted of pulling down the house of Mr Boggis, of New Turnstile. The keeper of Tothill Fields Bridewell would not suffer Jack Ketch to go among the other prisoners, lest they should tear him to pieces. In order that he might hang up his brother rioters, he was granted a pardon.

There are a number of contemporary reports, which add flesh to the gallows shown on Rocque's map of 1746. The *Grub Street Journal* of 7 May 1730 tells us that on 30 April, 'Yesterday Drummond and Shrimpton, lately hanged in chains on Stamford-hill, were removed with their gibbet to a remote part of the Common, near the place that Joseph Still was hanged in a like manner.'

The Gentleman's Magazine, in an 1856 edition, mentions that 'at an early date, even when St Giles was the regular place [of execution] … there were gallows and occasional executions at Shepherd's Bush, when Tybourn succeeded St Giles'.

There were gallows and gibbets scattered all over London, usually in prominent places to serve as a warning. Executions took place on Hampstead Heath quite near to where the Jack Straw's Castle Pub formerly stood near North End. The gallows were a rope strung between two large elm trees. The 1746 Rocque map also shows a double gibbet and gallows on the corner of Cricklewood Broadway (the Edgware Road) and what is now Chichele Road, NW2. The exact location is probably where Oaklands Road meets the Broadway. The gallows and gibbet on Shepherd's Bush Green stood at the eastern end maybe 100 yards south-west of Shepherd's Bush Underground station. The *Newgate Calendar* also mentions the execution of a highwayman at 'Porters Block' in St John Street, Smithfield.

The periphery of London was well populated by gallows, often remembered now by names such as Gallows Corner, or Gallows Hill. Aldenham near Watford has a hamlet called High Cross which had a gallows located on high ground, so as to be visible from St Albans. The listing and history of these sites would require another volume.

Notes

1 Marks, A., *Tyburn Tree: Its History and Annals* (London: Brown, Langham & Co, 1908), p. 292.

2 *Rotuli Hundredorum.*

3 Andrews, A., *The Eighteenth Century; or, Illustrations of the Manners and Customs of Our Grandfathers.* (London: Chapman & Hall, 1856), p. 269.

4 Marks, A., *Tyburn Tree.*

5 Montague, James, *The Old Bailey Chronicle*, vol. i (1783), pp. 51–3.

6 Hatton, E., *New View of London*, vol. i (1708), pp. 84–5.

7 Walford, E., 'Tyburn and Tyburnia' in *Old and New London: Volume 5* (1878), pp. 188–203.

8 Marks, A., *Tyburn Tree.*

9 Stubbs, William (ed.), *The Chronicle of the Reigns of Henry II and Richard I Commonly Known as Benedict of Peterborough* (London: HMSO, 1867), pp. 155–56; Stubbs, William (ed.), *Chronicles of Roger of Hoveden*, ii, p. 131.

10 Cotton, Bartholomew and H. R. Luard (ed.), *Historia Anglicana* (London: 1859), pp. 304–6; Riley, H. T. (ed.), 'The French Chronicle of London: Edward I' in *Chronicles of the Mayors and Sheriffs of London: 1188-1274* (1863), p. 295; Riley, H. T. (ed.) *Chronicles of William Rishanger* (Longman, Green, Longman, Roberts, and Green, 1865), p. 194.

11 Stow, John and Edmund Howes (ed.), *The Annales, or a Generall Chronicle of England, Begun First by Maister John Stow, and After him Continued and Augmented With Matters Forreyne, and Domestique, Auncient and Moderne, Vnto the Ende of this Present Yeere 1614*

(1631), pp. 303–4.

12 *Ibid.*, p. 365.

13 *Ibid.*, p. 385

14 Gairdner, James (ed.), *Gregory's Chronicle: 1461-1469. The Historical Collections of a Citizen of London in the Fifteenth Century* (London Camden Society, 1876) pp. 236–7.

15 Stow, *Annals*, p. 479.

16 Hall, Edward, *Hall's Chronicle: Containing the History of England, During the Reign of Henry the Fourth, and the Succeeding Monarchs, to the End of the Reign of Henry the Eighth, in Which are Particularly Described the Manners and Customs of those Periods. Carefully Collated with the Editions of 1548 and 1550* (London: J. Johnson, 1809), p. 491.

17 Kingsford, Charles L., *Chronicles of London* (Oxford: Clarendon Press, 1905), p. 256.

18 Stow, *Annals*, pp. 570–1.

19 Nichols, J. G., *Chronicle of the Grey Friars of London* (London: Camden Society, 1852), p. 203.

20 Hall, *Chronicle*, pp. 827–8; Nichols, *Chronicle*, p. 202; Wriothesley, Charles, *A Chronicle of England During the Reigns of the Tudors from AD 1485 to 1559*, i (1875), pp. 101–2.

21 Stow, *Annals*, p. 581.

22 Hall, *Chronicle*, p. 841.

23 Wriothesley, *Chronicle*, vol. i, p. 135; Holinshed, R., *Chronicles of England, Scotland and Ireland*, vol. iii, p. 954.

24 Hall, p. 842.

25 Stow, *Annals*, p. 583.

26 *Ibid.*, p. 586.

27 Nichols, *Chronicle*, p. 223.

28 Stow, *Annals*, p. 603.

29 *Ibid.*, p. 604.

30 *Ibid.*, pp. 666–7.

31 *Ibid.*, p. 694.

32 *Ibid.*

33 *Ibid.*

34 *Ibid.*

35 *Ibid.*, p. 698.

36 *Ibid.*, p. 628.

37 *Ibid.*, pp. 749–50.

38 *Ibid.*, pp. 764–5.

39 Acts of the Privy Council, New Series, xxviii., p. 187.

40 Stow, *Annals*, pp. 787.

41 *Ibid.*, p. 812.

42 *Ibid.*, p. 787.

43 Challoner, Richard, *Memoirs of Missionary Priests: and Other Catholics of Both Sexes, That Have Suffered Death in England on Religious Accounts, From the Year 1577 to 1684*, vol. ii (John T. Green, 1839), pp. 17–9.

44 *Ibid.*, p. 37.

45 *Ibid.*, pp. 39–44; Howell, J., and J. Jacobs, *Epistolae Ho-Elianae: The Familiar Letters of James Howell* (London: D. Nutt, 1890) p. 337.

46 Challoner, *Memoirs*, vol. ii, p. 20.

47 Stow, *Annals*, p. 1044.

48 Journals of the House of Lords, iv, pp. 662, 723.

49 Challoner, *Memoirs*, vol. ii, pp. 196–200.

50 Clarendon, Edward and William Macray (ed.), *The History of the Rebellion and Civil Wars in England Begun in the Year 1641*, vol. i. (1888), pp. 295–7; Hist. MSS. Comm., Report v. pt. i., p. 174.

51 'A Perfect narrative of the apprehension, tryal, and confession of the five several persons that were confederates in stealing the mace and the two privy purses from the Lord High-Chancellor of England as it was attested at the sessions held at Justice-Hall in the Old-Bayly, the seventh and eigth of March, anno. 1676/7' in Oldys, W. and J. Malham (eds.), *The Harleian Miscellany*, vol. viii, pp. 505–6.

52 Hist. MSS. Comm, Manuscripts of the Marquess of Ormonde, New series, vol. iv (1907).

53 Luttrell, Narcissus, *Brief Historical Relation of State Affairs*, vol. i., pp. 311–2.

54 *Ibid.*, vol. i, p. 378.

55 *Ibid.*, vol. i, pp. 374–87.

56 *Ibid.*, vol. ii, p. 103.

57 *Ibid.*, vol. ii, pp. 128–48.

58 *Ibid.*, vol. ii, p. 148.

59 *Ibid.*, vol. iii, p. 345.

60 *Ibid.*, vol. iii, p. 499.

61 *Ibid.*, vol. v, p. 623.

62 Montague, James, *The Old Bailey Chronicle*, vol. i, (1783) pp. 185–8.

63 Villette, *Annals of Newgate; or Malefactors Register*, vol. i, (J. Wenman, 1766), pp. 32–6.

64 *Ibid.*, vol. i, pp. 126–7, 16–24.

65 *Ibid.*, vol. i, pp. 394–428.

66 Walford, E., 'Tyburn and Tyburnia' in *Old and New London: Volume 2* (1878), pp. 380–404.

67 Marks, A., *Tyburn Tree*, p. 50.

68 Challoner, *Memoirs of Missionary Priests*, pp. 157–60.

69 Walford, E., 'Tyburn and Tyburnia' in *Old and New London: Volume 5* (1878), pp.188–203.

70 Shaw, Donald, *London in the Sixties, With a Few Digressions* (London: Everett, 1908).

71 Nichols, J. G. (ed.), 'Diary: 1554 (Jan – June)' in *The Diary of Henry Machyn: Citizen and Merchant-Taylor of London (1550–1563)* (Camden Society, 1848), pp. 50–66.

72 Foxe, John and John Cumming (ed.), *Book of Martyrs* (G. Virtue, 1844), p. 100.

73 Nichols, J. G. (ed.) 'Diary: 1554 (Jan – June)' in *The Diary of Henry Machyn: Citizen and Merchant-Taylor of London (1550–1563)* (Camden Society, 1848), p. 59.

Bibliography

Andrews, A., *The Eighteenth Century: or, Illustrations of the Manners and Customs of Our Grandfathers* (London: Chapman & Hall, 1856).

Bard, R., *Death in London: Places of Execution, Then and Now* (London: Historical, 2007).

Brooke, A. and D. Brandon, *Tyburn: London's Fatal Tree* (Long Preston: Magna, 2006).

Dickens, C., *Dickens's Dictionary of London 1888 : an Unconventional Handbook* (Moretonhampstead: Old House, 1993).

Foxe, John and John Cumming (ed.), *Book of Martyrs* (G. Virtue, 1844).

Linebaugh, P., *The London Hanged: Crime and Civil Society in the Eighteenth Century* (London: Verso, 2003).

Shaw, Donald, *London in the Sixties, With a Few Digressions* (London: Everett, 1908).

Marks, A., *Tyburn Tree: Its History and Annals* (London: Brown, Langham & Co, 1908).

Stow, J., *A Survey of London: Written in the Year 1598* (Stroud: Sutton Publishing, 2005).

Thornbury, W. and E. Walford, *Old and New London: Volume 5* (1878).

Also available from Amberley Publishing

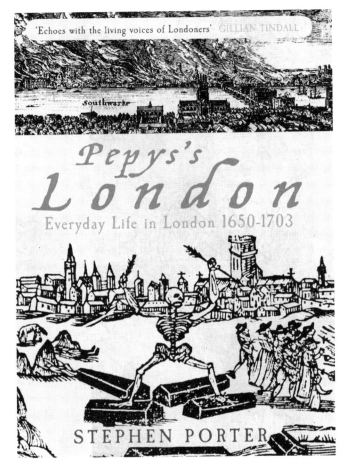

*Everyday life in the teeming metropolis during Pepys's time
in the city (c.1650-1703)*

'A fast-paced narrative with a real sense of history unfolding' GILLIAN TINDALL

Samuel Pepys's London was a turbulent, boisterous city, enduring the strains caused by foreign wars, the
Great Plague and the Great Fire, yet growing and prospering. The London of Wren, Dryden and Purcell was
also the city of Nell Gwyn, an orange seller in the theatre who became an actress and the king's mistress; of
'Colonel' Thomas Blood, who attempted to steal the crown jewels from the Tower and yet
escaped punishment; and of Titus Oates, whose invention of a Popish Plot provoked a major political crisis.

£10.99 Paperback
146 illustrations
256 pages
978-1-4456-0980-5

Available from all good bookshops or to order direct
Please call **01453-847-800**
www.amberleybooks.com

Also available from Amberley Publishing

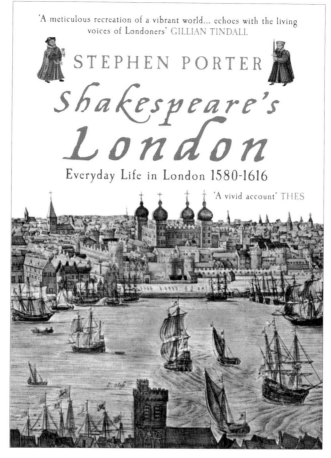

Everyday life in the teeming metropolis during William Shakespeare's time in the city (c.1580-1616), the height of Queen Elizabeth I's reign

'A vivid account' THES

'A lucid and cogent narrative of everyday life' SHAKESPEARE BIRTHPLACE TRUST

Shakespeare's London was a bustling, teeming metropolis that was growing so rapidly that the government took repeated, and ineffectual, steps to curb its expansion. From contemporary letters, journals and diaries, a vivid picture emerges of this fascinating city, with its many opportunities and also its persistent problems.

£9.99 Paperback
127 illustrations (45 colour)
304 pages
978-1-84868-200-9

Available from all good bookshops or to order direct
Please call **01453-847-800**
www.amberleybooks.com

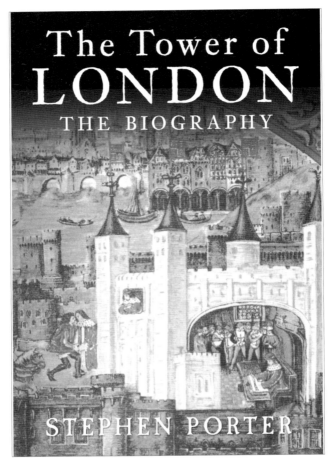

Also available from Amberley Publishing

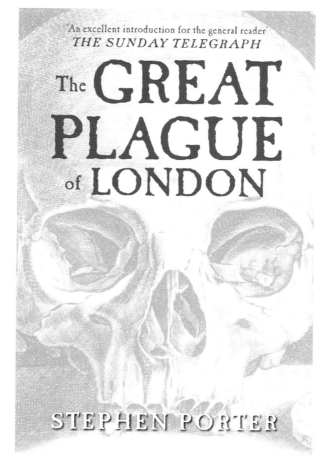

'An excellent introduction for the general reader'
THE SUNDAY TELEGRAPH

The bubonic plague epidemic which struck England in 1665-6 was responsible for the deaths of almost a third of London's population. Its sheer scale was overwhelming and it was well-recorded, featuring in the works of Pepys and Defoe and described in terrible detail in the contemporary Bills of Mortality. Stephen Porter describes the disease and how people at the time thought it was caused. He gives details of the treatments available (such as they were) and evokes its impact on the country. We will probably never know the reasons for the disappearance of the bubonic plague from England after 1665. What is clear is the fascination the subject still holds.

£10.99 Paperback
61 illustrations
192 pages
978-1-4456-0773-6

Available from all good bookshops or to order direct
Please call **01453-847-800**
www.amberleybooks.com

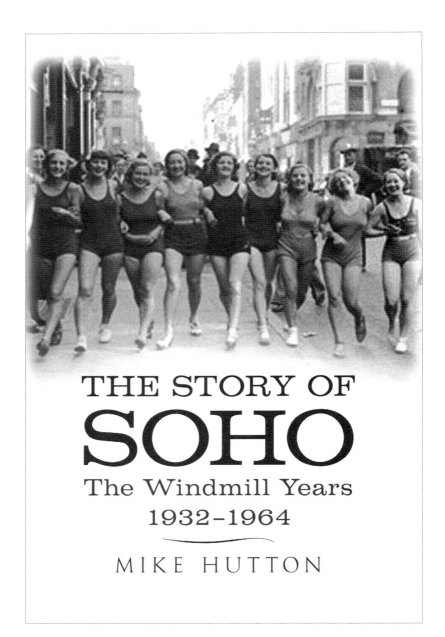

THE STORY OF
SOHO
The Windmill Years
1932–1964

MIKE HUTTON

Also available from Amberley Publishing

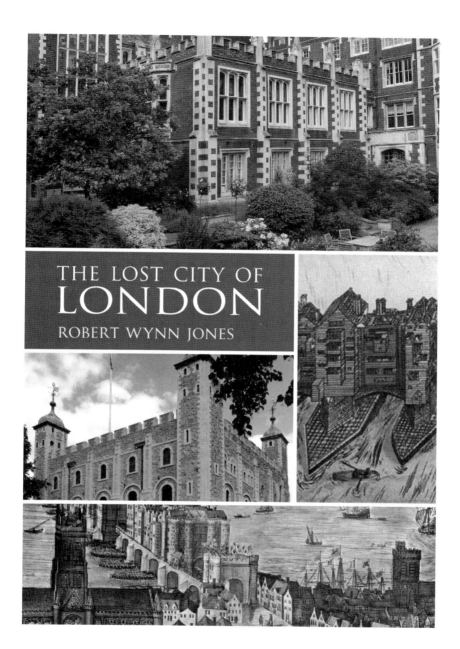

THE LOST CITY OF
LONDON
ROBERT WYNN JONES

Also available from Amberley Publishing

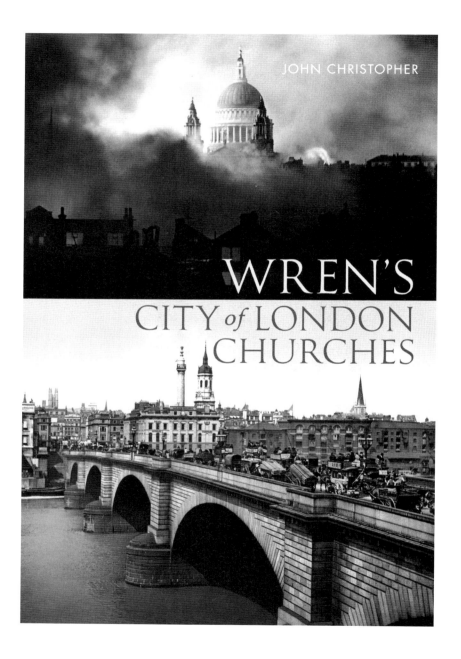

Available from all good bookshops or to order direct
Please call **01453-847-800**
www.amberleybooks.com

Also available from Amberley Publishing

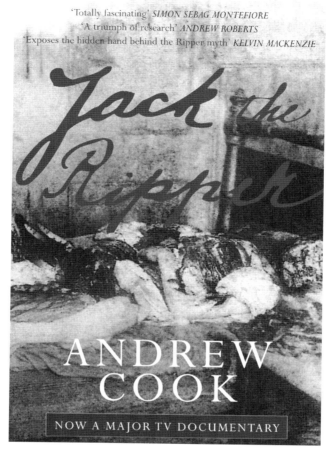

Also available from Amberley Publishing

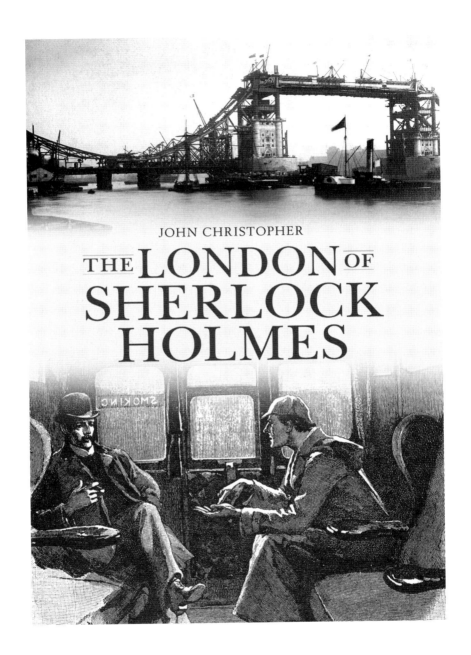

JOHN CHRISTOPHER

THE LONDON OF
SHERLOCK
HOLMES